EFFECTIVE HANDLING OF MANIPULATIVE PERSONS

ABOUT THE AUTHOR

John D. Lentz, D. Min. is the Chief Chaplain at the Kentucky Correctional Institution for Women. He is also an Adjunct Professor in Pastoral Care and Counseling at the Louisville Presbyterian Theological Seminary where he earned both his M. Div. and D. Min. degrees. John earned his undergraduate degree from the University of Louisville. He is a member of or holds credentials from the following organizations: American Correctional Association, American Association for Marriage and Family Therapists, American Association of Pastoral Counselors, Association for Clinical Pastoral Education, the National Association for Clergy Hypnotherapists, the Kentucky Association for Specialists in Group Work, and the Louisville Union Presbytery.

John and his wife Debra live, along with their two children Seth and Stacey, in the log cabin they built together.

EFFECTIVE HANDLING
OF
MANIPULATIVE PERSONS

By

JOHN D. LENTZ

CHARLES C THOMAS • PUBLISHER
Springfield • Illinois • U.S.A.

Published and Distributed Throughout the World by
CHARLES C THOMAS • PUBLISHER
2600 South First Street
Springfield, Illinois 62794-9265

This book is protected by copyright. No part of
it may be reproduced in any manner without
written permission from the publisher.

© *1989 by* CHARLES C THOMAS • PUBLISHER
ISBN 0-398-05555-6
Library of Congress Catalog Card Number: 88-39519

With THOMAS BOOKS *careful attention is given to all details of manufacturing and design. It is the Publisher's desire to present books that are satisfactory as to their physical qualities and artistic possibilities and appropriate for their particular use.* THOMAS BOOKS *will be true to those laws of quality that assure a good name and good will.*

Printed in the United States of America
Q-R-3

Library of Congress Cataloging-in-Publication Data
Lentz, John D.
  Effective handling of manipulative persons / by John D. Lentz.
    p. cm.
  Bibliography: p.
  Includes index.
  ISBN 0-398-05555-6
  1. Prison psychology.   2. Manipulative behavior.   I. Title.
HV6098.L46 1989
365'.6'019—dc 19   88-39519
                                                                      CIP

This book is dedicated to the work of Clarence Y. Barton, David A. Steere, and the late George F. Bennett whose brilliance in working with people is only matched by their genuineness.

ACKNOWLEDGMENTS

I WANT TO THANK Jane Thompson, KCIW psychologist, for the use of the coauthored Behavioral Option Chart, her continuing support, and invaluable expertise. I would like to thank the Kentucky Department of Corrections, Office of Training for their generosity of materials and time. I also want to thank the KCIW volunteer visitors, Clinical Pastoral Education students and staff members who have given generously of their time and comments in reading this material. I am indebted to Dot Matthews and LaVerne Alexander for typing and editing this manuscript. In similar fashion I am appreciative of the work Tim Norris did in illustrating the chapter headings. Louis Weeks, David Steere, Bill Gorman, Clarence Barton, and George Bennett gave me invaluable encouragement and ideas to complete this project and deserve recognition for their efforts. I am also grateful to my family—Debra, my wife, and to Seth and Stacey, my children—for their support and understanding as I worked on this book. Finally, I am grateful to the inmates of the Kentucky Correctional Institution for Women who have taught me about manipulation, and who continue to help me understand the complexities of relationships and manipulation.

CONTENTS

Page

Introduction 3

Chapter

    1. Protecting Ourselves 9
    2. Discovering What Is Expected of Us 19
    3. Discovering Ways the Manipulator Is Not Taking Responsibility ... 33
    4. Giving Back Responsibility 45
    5. Taking Care of Yourself 65

Appendix 1. Theological Foundation 73
Appendix 2. Theoretical Foundation 79

Bibliography 89
Chart 93
Index 97

EFFECTIVE HANDLING OF MANIPULATIVE PERSONS

Introduction

EFFECTIVE HANDLING OF MANIPULATIVE PERSONS

THIS PROJECT AROSE from seeing the difficulties that people who were beginning work in corrections were having in coping with the manipulative behavior of inmates. Most people seemed to experience manipulation as a personal act against them. As a consequence, they felt betrayed and hurt that people whom they had come to trust had violated their trust intentionally.

People who work in corrections are assaulted with a barrage of manipulative ploys from inmates. The manipulative and self-destructive behaviors of inmates tend to elicit similar responses which are neither helpful to inmates nor employees. The most frequently asked questions from staff members, inmates' volunteer visitors and students which involve manipulation are: "How do I deal with my own feelings?" In an informal survey of correctional officers all were asked, "What has been the most difficult situation for you to deal with in corrections?" All respondents cited situations in which they were or felt manipulated. Eleven of the twelve were manipulated by inmates, one by staff. These difficult situations involved repetitive and self-destructive behaviors and statements by inmates. Yet good officers, even those with experience, appeared to feel the effects of the subtle and not so subtle manipulative gestures of inmates. Frequently, talented officers left corrections, giving the impression they believed they could no longer cope with the stress and abuse. Volunteers appeared to be even more vulnerable to being manipulated, and there seemed to be few ways of equipping them short of the "sink or swim" method, in spite of compulsory training for all volunteers. What I believed would help was for everyone to have access to information about manipulation and more options for effectively dealing with manipulation.

The intention of this book is to provide useful tools. That is, to provide information about manipulation and to offer principles and techniques that are effective in handling manipulation. Effectiveness is thought of as being both therapeutic for inmates and protective of the officer's emotional self. The therapeutic value of the options offered is that they do not contribute to the cycle of self-destructive behavior of the manipulators. The options are intended to be emotionally safeguarding of the officer's feelings by a variety of methods. The book is written for the use of staff members, volunteers, and anyone interested in manipulation. Furthermore, it is intended to stimulate the reader's creativity and to help him or her recognize the effective methods she/he already uses. Although some of the information may be new, the techniques are ones we all use while relating to people we like. What is different is applying these same methods of relating to people who, at times, try our patience. All of the options are intended to be easily applied and usable by people without training in psychology. Substance abuse counselors and management personnel will especially find the techniques helpful. In fact, most people find that the options are useful in a variety of settings.

The material presented is based upon the Bible, a variety of counseling approaches, and personal experience. It is written to illustrate some ways in which theology and psychology can be integrated. In doing so, the first Appendix illustrates the theological basis for understanding manipulation and the methods of intervention that are included in the book itself. In a similar fashion, Appendix Two reflects the theoretical and psychological methods that are applications of the theological stance and are used in the book.

> Behold I send you out as sheep in the midst of wolves, so be as wise as serpents and as innocent as doves (Matthew 10:160).[1]

Effective dealing with manipulative persons means just what Jesus said, being as wise as the manipulators and yet not doing any harm. Sheep in the midst of wolves are vulnerable and so are we.[2] What follows is designed to help us in dealing with the manipulative and abusive situations in which we have chosen to work. In other words, it is designed to help us be able to remain as sheep in the midst of wolves.

Working inside a prison is not easy. We constantly deal with role conflict and stress.[3] We also have to deal with the element of fear.[4] Most of us are wary of being conned by inmates continuously.[5] Our jobs are more than knowing how to keep the inmates from breaking the rules or from beating the system. Although our primary purpose is to keep incarcerated persons incarcerated, our main jobs are to work with inmates in order that change may take place.[6] The welfare of ourselves, the other officers, inmates, and the community are all dependent upon change happening as people are incarcerated. The institution and all those involved are counting on the orderly and safe running of the institution.

If prison personnel are able to de-escalate possible inflammatory situations, then the safety of all is increased. Furthermore, the safer the institution, both emotionally and physically, the better chance of inmates deciding to change destructive behaviors toward oneself and others. Psychotherapists are often heard to say about therapy, "Our task is to create a safe place in which to change." The same applies to corrections. We need to create an atmosphere that is safe physically and emotionally. The best way for us to do that is by feeling safe ourselves. Emotions can be passed on like footballs, or hot potatoes. Anyone who has witnessed the emotional tone of an institution change within a matter of hours knows how volatile tension and fear can be inside a prison. Furthermore, staff are vulnerable to the wave of emotion and tension and can often contribute unwittingly. It is common knowledge that one danger in working with depressed persons is becoming depressed oneself. However, the depression, fear, or general uneasiness can be passed back and forth between inmates and staff. We would all do well to take note from recent findings in the supervision of student psychotherapists. Studies indicated that supervisors of therapists greatly effected the patient's behavior even though they had little or no contact. The reason is that supervised folks tend to treat the people they supervise or work with in either the same or the opposite of the way they are treated.[7] In other words supervision works a lot like a combination shot in pool. The first ball strikes the second which in turn strikes the third into the pocket. In prison we frequently see this phenomenon when there are shift changes and administrative personnel changes. Often the entire mood of the institution changes as key administrative personnel are replaced. On a daily basis the mood of particular areas is altered by who the officer is in charge. Captains regularly place calm officers in tense areas to help calm the inmates. If we accept this premise then we must also recognize that the constant razzing and hurtful things that are said, build in security problems for inmates and staff. We react to some of the put-downs, implied slurs, and emotional abuse that goes on inside and is directed toward us.

Of course, we develop ways to deal with manipulation, abuse, and its emotional toll, or do we? Anyone who has worked in corrections for any length of time has had inmates say hurtful things to them, and often we like to act as if it doesn't hurt or that it doesn't bother us. We often tell ourselves that we can't let what inmates say bother us. It is true that those who stay find ways to protect themselves. However, even for the well-defended emotionally, inmates can say, on occasion, just the right thing, and then we end up spending hours nursing our bruised ego or going over and over the difficult situation.[8] Let's face it. Inmates spend a lot of time reading people in order to con them. They can often find our Achilles' heel.

The intent of this book is to show means for ensuring everyone's safety by illustrating ways to de-escalate potentially angry situations before a blowup, and for these ways to be therapeutic and helpful for the inmates at the same time. Therapeutic in a sense that our reactions do not contribute to the inmate's cycle of self and other destructive behavior.

Manipulation uses an unspoken message to generate its power. It is this message that is conveyed with or without words that is spoken between the lines of a conversation that is manipulation. There are four principles underlying the methods used in this book to deal with manipulative ploys. They are essential in an effective handling of manipulators, because it is our attitude that greatly determines how safe we are and how effective we will be. The four principles are as follows: (1) the underlying goal of the manipulator's behavior needs attention; (2) our response ideally should not contribute to the person's cycle of self-destructive behavior; (3) our response is most effective when it recognizes the value of the inmate and provides safety for us; and (4) our response should return responsibility to the inmate.

A clear example of this occurs in Mark 12:12-17. In that passage some religious leaders wanted to entrap Jesus, and his answer in the passage illustrates the principles above. Jesus did three things in the exchange that we can learn from. He found how the manipulators were not taking personal responsibility and he gave it back to them without taking the problem they planned to give him. In discovering what was expected, Jesus listened to the unspoken message which was implied but not spoken. The religious manipulators sought to entrap him and had set him up with a compliment and a question designed to appear with only two answers.

> And they came and said to him, "Teacher, we know that you are true, and care for no man; for you do not regard the position of men, but truly teach the way of God. Is it lawful to pay taxes to Caesar, or not?[9]

Both the obvious answers were a trap. To answer "yes" would have angered and displeased the people wanting relief from Roman rule, and to answer "no" also would have angered the Roman authorities. Government doesn't like people being encouraged not to pay taxes. The unspoken message was "we got you."

Jesus found the way that the manipulators or religious leaders were not taking responsibility. They were not taking responsibility on two levels. First, they were not up front with their attack of Jesus. Secondly they were not showing any allegiance to God by their question. They asked a question that had nothing to do with God, although it seemed to on the surface. Jesus gave back responsibility to the religious leaders by answering the unspoken message.

By stating "Who do you put me to the test?" he has already brought into the open the unspoken message of the religious leaders. The rest of his answer, "Render unto Caesar the things that are Caesar's, and to God the things that are God's," gave them back responsibility. By pointing out the image on the coin, he reminded them that they were made in the image of God and that they had responsibility to God first. His answer allowed them to confront themselves with their own behavior. It also avoided the trap which they had set for him.

Thus Jesus spoke to the underlying goal of the manipulator, did not contribute to the cycle by playing into the trap, allowed respect for the manipulators by letting their own words confront them, and returned responsibility to the manipulators while avoiding the trap they had set for him.

Another example of manipulation is what you just encountered. It is more subtle. Notice that an example from the Christian Bible was used rather than one from a prison setting. You have had a response to reading that example. That response was generated by the choice of example and your feelings about Jesus, no matter whether they are positive or negative.

There were two other conscious reasons that the passage from the Bible was chosen. Both are manipulative and have to do with teaching about manipulation. Neither of the other reasons has to do with "winning converts to Jesus." By the end of the book you will be able to guess the reasons.

There are five steps to this approach of dealing with manipulators. The five steps are: (1) protecting ourselves; (2) discovering what is expected of us; (3) discovering how the manipulator isn't taking responsibility; (4) giving back responsibility; and (5) taking care of yourself. It is not important to memorize these principles or steps. They are to give clarity to the process that is discussed. Dealing with manipulation is a lot like learning to ride a bike or swimming. Principles and steps can help us figure out what we are doing that isn't working. Yet while biking or swimming we don't often think of the principles involved, we simply keep our balance and ride or swim.

NOTES

[1] *The Bible*, Matthew 10:16.

[2] Eric D. Poole and Robert M. Regoli, "Work Relations and Cynicism Among Prison Guards," *Criminal Justice and Behavior*, Vol. 7, No. 3 (September, 1980), p. 305.

[3] Carroll M. Brodsky, "Work Stress in Correctional Institutions," *Journal of Prison and Jail Health*, Vol. 2, No. 2 (Fall/Winter, 1982), p. 79.

[4] Ronald Black, "Stress and the Correctional Officer," *Police Stress* (February, 1982), p. 12.

[5] Eric D. Poole and Robert M. Regoli, "Alienation in Prison," *Criminology*, Vol. 19, No. 2 (August, 1981), p. 265.

[6] "Annual Planning Document for Kentucky Correctional Institute for Women," Pewee Valley, KY, prepared by Betty Kassulke, Warden, and department heads, 4th education (1983-84), p. 4.

[7] Margery J. G. Doehrman. "Parallel Process in Supervision and Psychotherapy," *Bulletin of the Menninger Clinic*, Vol. 40, No. 1 (January, 1976), pp. 71-72.

[8] Black, p. 12.

[9] *The Bible*, Mark 12:14.

Chapter 1

PROTECTING OURSELVES

PEOPLE NEW TO corrections often seek to protect themselves from the manipulation of inmates by either trusting or almost believing something sinister is happening always. Their actions declare loudly on which position they have decided. The trusting ones will get burned quickly, and so will the mistrusting ones. The only difference is that the person who believes that being on guard for manipulation will save them gets taken in a meaner sort of way. The result may be the same, but the trusting person isn't despised, he is simply not taken seriously.

The way this usually gets played out is that the truster befriends the first people who reach out. After a brief close relationship the truster realizes that everyone isn't to be trusted and is usually sad that someone he trusted treated him so badly. The mistruster is severe in applying the rules and strains at a knat, while a resenting manipulator gleefully enjoys putting one over at the mistruster's expense. It is really simple, if you know that I will get interested in and take seriously any minor occurrence, all you have to do to distract me is create some minor bending of the rules that I can't do more than complain about. All the while you have done whatever else that you wanted to do while I was busy lecturing about a minor rule.

Our attitude is vital in protecting ourselves. Attitudes determine our effectiveness, can be a measure of our ability to maintain relationships, and indicate our susceptibility to stress and manipulation. Our attitude determines our effectiveness in the area of perception. One study of jail inmates and correctional officers found that the more severe a situation the more likely each was to blame the other.[1] The same study found that both inmates and guards believed that they were blamed more than they actually were.[2] In other words, if our attitude toward a situation is fear of being blamed, we may have a hard time being accurate in interpreting the details of what others' behavior means.

Blaming others when we feel responsible has long been recognized to be a means of self-protection. We all use it even if it doesn't do anything more than assuage our egos. If fate, frustration, or some other outside factor can be blamed, then inmates tend to react more negatively when officers place blame with them.[3] That is pretty understandable. Who of us likes someone pointing out our mistakes when we are trying hard to blame it on our dumb car, the weather, or some other person. However, the attitude of blaming the system carries with it a warning. One researcher found that when correctional officers were blaming the system, they were likely in burn-out.[4] Blaming the system, inmates or environmental factors is neither helpful to our attitude, nor to us in the long run. When we shift blame we also know in the back of our minds that we are doing so, and we try all the harder to escape our feeling of responsibility. Facing our own mistakes squarely inspires respect, both for ourself as well as from others.

Our attitude of blaming may speak more directly about our relationships and our ability to maintain them than about our guilt or innocence. One study found that the more cynicism the guards had the more likely their relationships with their supervisors were disrupted.[5] The truth of this correlation is simple. The less trust I have of my supervisor the more cynical I will become, because the more I believe that people will treat me badly, the more they probably will. It becomes a self-fulfilling prophecy.

Fears in general are notorious for running our lives. That is especially true in dealing with manipulative people, because they will detect the fear and exploit it. The fear is exploited primarily because a person cannot or will not acknowledge the fear and deal with it in another manner. One male officer I know, had to resign in part because he was afraid to discuss or acknowledge to himself that he found some of the inmates very attractive. Instead, he attempted to deny that he was human and hoped the inmates wouldn't talk to him about sex. He felt guilty that he found women attractive that he wasn't supposed to have that kind of feeling about. The inmates picked up on his fear and were as seductive with him as possible. Finally, he couldn't take any more and quit. Fortunately, he knew enough to leave rather than act out his fear with one of the inmates.

Most of us realize that animals can sense fear; so can people. Inmates can easily sense what we are afraid of and use that knowledge to manipulate us by using our fear as a lever to control our behavior. Few officers who remain in corrections make the mistake of letting inmates know that they fear being disliked. Obviously we cannot eliminate a fear that we have simply by telling ourselves not to feel it. However, what we tell ourselves and others is instrumental in creating our attitudes and feelings.

It is a radical idea that we actually have control over how we feel.[6] For example, if you will, imagine that you are on a crowded bus and you are standing in the aisle. As you were getting on, you noticed a woman and a young child sitting behind you. All of a sudden, you feel a sharp jab in your back and you think, "that kid must have poked me with his mother's umbrella." You don't say anything, because the bus is crowded. You go along for a little while longer, and all of a sudden, you are jabbed in the back twice more and both times it hurts. You turn around in anger to tell the mother what she ought to do with her child. Just as you turn around, you realize that the woman is the one who jabbed you in the back and that she jabbed you because she is blind.

Do you feel the same as you did before you realized that she was blind? Probably not. Is there a difference other than what you have told yourself? Where did your anger go? What we tell ourselves does decide how we will feel and what our attitudes will be toward the other person.

What we tell ourselves about the inmates' manipulation is therefore of crucial importance. One psychoanalytic view of manipulation that is generally held by people who set themselves up has four parts. These parts are: conflict of goals; intention; deception and insincerity; and a feeling of having put one over.[7] Most of us will consciously agree that manipulation has these four elements. They should like the way we think of manipulation. However, deciding whether a person's behavior is manipulative by these guidelines is not that simple. First, we have to prove at least to ourselves that the act was through conscious intention. The problem is deciding when a person's behavior is conscious and when that behavior is out of his awareness or unconscious.[8] To truly be able to know if an inmate's manipulative-like behavior is conscious, we would almost have to read his/her mind.

While it is true that some situations involve manipulation that has been schemed out to a tight-fitting plan, these are in the minority. Believing that all manipulation is thought-out is generous to inmates' ability to use forethought. The truth is that if they thought that much about the future, many wouldn't be in prison. Inmates are notorious for having no impulse control, not for elaborate planning.

Furthermore, by mind reading that actions have only conscious awareness, we invite bad feelings for ourselves and tend to escalate encounters with the inmates. Few of us can feel manipulated and continue to like the person who has intentionally gotten the best of us. Ordinarily, we are angry with the person. Because of our anger, we want to retaliate and punish the inmate who has manipulated us. From this position of righteous anger we invite further bad feelings, in part because we are usually determined to make the other person pay or change. We know that we are right and that the other person will see it our way, because we are stronger, brighter, more in control, etc. Wrong. The righteous position of stronger authority through control or sheer strength is the weakest position, and can be thwarted every time a person is willing to prove the point.

One resident demonstrated the above truth over a period of time. The woman, having broken institutional rules, was placed in the cell block. Thus, the institution took the "top dog"[9] position, and the inmate gladly took the "underdog" position. The institution was determined that she would not continue breaking the rules. She would prove us wrong. While in the cell block, she was determined to show us who was boss. Taking a small container, she scooped whatever was in her toilet bowl and began throwing it at officers who walked past her cell. The officers understandably didn't like that. The institution's solution was to put up a plexiglass shield across her door. This, of course, would keep her from throwing excretement on officers—you would think—but would it restrain her behavior? She was much more creative. She proceeded to tear the toilet out of the wall, flooding the entire upstairs cell block. After several more rounds with her and the institution, a neighboring institution decided that they could control her behavior. KCIW was very glad to allow the other institution this control, so she was moved. At the new institution, she proceeded to tear toilets out of the wall, again causing flooding. The new institution did not approve either. Although she had broken handcuffs before, they handcuffed her to her cell door. No, she wasn't superwoman, but she knew a trick to breaking handcuffs.

Any rational person would believe that this "top dog" position would, in fact, keep her controlled. Wrong. She simply proceeded to urinate and defecate on herself. The officers who had to clean her up did not like it. The new institution then thought that they had the perfect solution: they handcuffed her hand and foot to the cell door naked. When she urinated or defecated on herself, they would just hose her down, presenting little problem for their officers. However, the problem was that she sued the institution and won.

I believe that she also proved another point that correctional people are often ready to affirm, that is, we run the institution, because the inmates allow us to. Pointing out an inmate's mistakes in a punitive fashion with anger in our voice may in fact lead to increased disruptive behavior and manipulation.[10] Many manipulators enjoy getting the authorities angry, and can spot someone trying to take the top dog position in a second. Using humor or a sense of humor when pointing out the "con" is unsettling to the manipulator, because it shows one's expertise. Sometimes this actually seduces the manipulator into wondering what you know. Getting angry says that you are not any smarter than any of the other people they have bested all their life. Letting yourself be conned destroys credibility.[11]

The word manipulate or manipulation carries with it negative baggage. Most of us, when we think of being manipulated or people who manipulate, have a disdain for that type of behavior. However, if we are honest with ourselves we know that we are manipulative in relationships.[12] Webster's Dictionary defines manipulate as "(1) to work, operate, or treat with or as with the hand or hands; handle or use, especially with skill; (2) to manage or control artfully or by shrewd use of influence, often in an unfair or fraudulent way."[13] The fact is that we highly praise folks who can manipulate us. We pay them money to entertain us on the screen. We read books because they keep us interested and engrossed in the story. There is manipulation which is positive and invites the person being manipulated or enticed to have increased options. And there is manipulation which seeks to limit the other person's options, thus giving the first person control. It is to our advantage to recognize the inmates' manipulations that seek to control our behavior as simply ineffective communication. Operating with the belief that other people need to be treated like objects and controlled points to low self-esteem.

Our attitudes are reflected in what we do and what we say, as well as how we feel. For this reason many people take karate or judo lessons, even though they don't want to fight. They want to feel confident. Deodorant commercials have capitalized on this basic desire to feel confident. Knowing where your own value comes from is the same type of thing, only better. It doesn't wear off and you don't have to spend years learning to kick, punch, or throw your opponent. Having confidence in ourselves comes from trusting ourselves and the source of our value. In part that means being rigorously honest with ourselves. It also means knowing some manipulation safeguards.

Knowing where our value comes from is important. The better we feel about ourselves, the more likely it is that we will not be threatened by harmful things that others say to us. Furthermore, knowing who and what is important to us is part of taking care of our spiritual, emotional, and physical needs. It also means keeping a constant eye on those needs. Our effectiveness often reflects how well we have taken care of ourselves. Everyone knows how grouchy some of us get if we don't get enough sleep, rest, or our spiritual needs met. Any weakness that we have and are not aware of will probably be brought to our attention sooner or later with or without good intentions of our hearing the news. Our believed value is the foundation for any self-protection package.

By avoiding talking about any person who is not present, we communicate to an inmate that we are trustworthy and that we won't talk about them when they are not around us. True, you might think that rule cuts down on the tips you get about others. I find that it merely cuts down on the manipulation and games that get played. Tactfully letting someone know that we won't discuss a third person can be easily done. It can range from simply not mentioning the other person and only talking about how the inmate whom we are with feels, to directly confronting the person, if repeatedly asked for comments about a third party. Folks who don't follow this rule with their peers don't have anyone they can trust.

A couple of ways that I ensure this rule for myself is that whenever a person mentions a third person's name, I hold up my hand and ask for no names. Another way I let people know my intention is to simply state it: "I will talk with you about you and with other people about themselves." Although this position means foregoing those juicy tidbits about others, it is helpful. Furthermore, talking about the other person won't help anybody to change. Besides, if you will let me tell you what someone said about you, t-h-e-n you do not know whether I am saying it to you, or if the third person said it, or even if I'm repeating something I heard, but I also want to say it to you.

Learn as much as you can about manipulation from whatever sources are available. While you can think of some other sources, commercials on television are a wellspring of knowledge about manipulation. One way to let them teach you is to detect what the advertisers are really saying between the lines of what their advertisement says. Often the message they want us to get has nothing to do with the actual words spoken. Frequently, advertisements imply that if we use their product we will become glamorous, slender, wealthy, sexy, etc. These unspoken messages are never stated because, if spoken, everyone could see through the dishonesty. Truth in advertising often does not apply to what is implied or unspoken.

By taking the attitude of desiring instruction in manipulation, we reduce greatly the hurtful effects that being manipulated can have. For instance, when taken, we can rejoice at knowing another way of being manipulated and therefore figure out ways to stop it in the future. The book of Proverbs has many pieces of advice for us concerning our willingness to be corrected. Chapter 13 verse 18 states, "For the man (woman) who rejects discipline, poverty and disgrace. For the man (woman) who accepts correction, order."[14] When we recognize we have been had or conned, we can understand that as being disciplined. We have not acted or reacted as positively as we could. By simply being angry, we reject the learning that could take place.

Probably the most important thing in protecting ourselves, besides knowing where our value comes from, is understanding the language of the unspoken messages. Often it is by not responding to the unspoken message, or by responding to it directly and not indirectly as it was given, that gets us in trouble. Suppose that an attractive inmate is coming on to you in nonverbal ways. There isn't anything to document; the seduction is more through looks and gestures. Confront this person coming on to you directly and you will be accused yourself. Fail to address the message and you will be maneuvered whether it means being seduced or not. The only safe and sensible way is through the unspoken language of a message between the lines.

Messages that are said through the unspoken language which are belittling, demeaning, or disrespectful are sometimes called discounts.[15] The following is an example of discounting. This is part of an actual letter a woman was writing from prison to her mother. After talking with me, she decided not to send the letter, but agreed to allow it to be used to teach others about discounting. I thought it was a slick way of helping her to realize what she was saying to her mother and to get a good example to teach discounting to others. See how many of the unspoken messages or discounts you can recognize.

> Dear Mom and family, How is everyone? I am fine, I guess, considering that I feel no one cares enough for me to write me. Mommy, after all we've been through together, you've never let me down until now. What are you trying to do? Drive me crazy or something? This morning at breakfast I broke down and almost cried in front of everyone, I ran upstairs to my bed. She came up and told me not to worry, that I would be hearing from you soon. Is she right? Will I hear from my family? I sure do hope and pray so. Mom, what is it that I have done so awful, terribly wrong? Why can't you love me like you used to? No matter how you have turned against me, I will always love you. Can't you find it in your heart to forgive me and show me that you do care for me? Please, I beg of you to at least help me.

The letter goes on for five pages of phrases and discounting like this. The letter illustrates some basic principles about discounting. Discounts always go both ways. In other words, when we discount someone else we are at the same time discounting ourselves. A discount is usually present when more than one message is intended to be communicated, while another thought or subject is desired to be kept secret. Discounts happen frequently because of some unspoken rule or fear that we have to communicate directly. For instance, this woman was angry with her mother. We can also recognize that she wanted her mother to write her. She was afraid to speak openly of her anger because her mother might write or visit even less. So her anger comes out in her words of manipulation, that seek to have control over her mother, to coerce her into visiting.

The first discount comes in the second sentence in which she implies that her mother does not care enough for her to write. There are discounts in all of the other sentences. The way a discount affects the person writing or speaking the discount is by implying that he/she does not have some ability, value, or power that all intact human beings have. Were you able to recognize all of the discounts?

SUMMARY

In this section we saw how our attitude can influence the level of blame we feel. We also saw how this affects our likelihood to blame the inmates. In addition, we saw that the more likely we are to blame others, the higher the stress that we are likely to feel.

What we tell ourselves was covered, as well as how this can set up a "no win" situation in one of two major ways. That is, our feelings are influenced by what we tell ourselves. Furthermore, our need to have someone change or behave can create a situation in which we cannot win.

As a result, we discussed one manner of understanding manipulation that allowed for a realistic method of self protection. This position held that manipulation can be both positive and negative. The difference was whether the act attempted to take away or give control to the other person. Or in other words, does the manipulation increase or decrease the other person's options?

In keeping ourselves protected we covered a list of protective behaviors that included the following methods: (a) always verify an inmate's story when possible; (b) drain any hostility with another professional and not with the inmate; (c) know where our own value comes from; (d) avoid talking about people not present; (e) know as much as possible about manipulation; (f) watch for the unspoken message; and (g) remember that discounts go both ways, toward us and to the person giving us the discount.

In the next section we will cover the ways we can discover what is expected of us. The better we are able to protect ourselves, the more capable we will be utilizing the other techniques in this work.

NOTES

[1] Dorothy K. Kagehiro and Carol M. Werner, "Divergent Perception of Jail Inmates and Correctional Officers: The 'Blame the Other--Expect to be Blamed' Effect," *Journal of Applied Social Psychology* (1981, 11, 66), p. 519.
[2] Ibid., p. 508.
[3] Ibid., p. 526.
[4] Carroll M. Brodsky, "Work Stress in Correctional Institutions," *Journal of Prison and Jail Health*, Vol. 2, No. 2 (Fall/Winter, 1982), p. 79.
[5] Eric D. Poole and Robert M. Regoli, "Work Relations and Cynicism Among Prison Guards," *Criminal Justice and Behavior*, Vol. 7, No. 3 (September, 1980), p. 305.
[6] Albert Ellis and Robert A. Harper, *A New Guide to Rational Living* (Englewood Cliffs, NJ: Prentice-Hall, Inc., 1957), pp. 9-12.
[7] Ben Bursten, M.D., *The Manipulator: A Psychoanalytic View* (New Haven and London: Yale University Press, 1973), p. 8.
[8] Ibid., p. 26.
[9] Fredrick S. Perls, *Gestalt Therapy Verbatim* (New York: Bantam Books, Inc., 1974 [first printed by Real People Press in 1969], p. 19.
[10] Heinz L. Ansbacher and Rowena R. Ansbacher, *The Individual Psychology of Alfred Adler* (New York: Harper and Row Publishers, 1956), p. 423.
[11] George F. Bennett, *When They Ask for Bread* (Atlanta: John Knox Press, 1978), p. 93.
[12] Ibid., p. 88.
[13] Webster's Dictionary, s.v., "manipulate."
[14] *The Bible*, Proverbs 13:18.
[15] Jacqui Lee Schiff, *Cathexis Reader* (New York: Harper & Row, 1975), p. 14.

Chapter 2

DISCOVERING WHAT IS EXPECTED OF US

DISCOVERING WHAT IS expected of us is a crucial task in working with people.[1] While there are a variety of ways ranging from the comical to the absurd, the easiest way is to simply ask.[2] Asking the other person what they want from us may, in fact, lay bare the distinction between whether they are seeking to manipulate us or are asking for factual information, feedback, advice, etc. While inmates may simply want an escape from boredom, they may also want simply to be recognized.

There are a lot of theories and theoreticians expounding reasons for behavior or misbehavior. One theory that is easy to understand without hours of training, and seems to be reasonably useful, lists four goals of misbehavior: attention, power, revenge, and display of inadequacy. Manipulative behaviors can most often be understood as relating to these four goals for misbehavior.[3]

A primary measure of the truthfulness of a theory is in whether it is useful. Does the theory provide a useful way of understanding behavior? Who knows if this or any theory about behavior is accurate, in any ultimate sense? What is important is whether the information it contains helps us work with people and especially to understand what their behavior is asking of us.

While asking someone verbally what they want from us is prudent, it also does not always work. People don't always know what their behavior is eliciting. Nor does everyone know what they want. The four areas of attention, power, revenge, and display of inadequacy are useful because they arrange a multitude of misbehavior into four distinct groups that can be utilized for developing methods of handling behaviors in that grouping. In fact, that is what much of this book is about.

Often, how we are feeling is an excellent clue to what is being asked of us. The four areas of misbehavior all tend to elicit different feelings from us on a regular basis. Most people can and will be able to identify with the following common responses to the areas of misbehavior.

Some common behaviors that could be understood as seeking attention are showing off, teasing, making cute comments, asking for special privileges, looking disgusted, asking lots of questions, and disagreeing. When an inmate is doing some attention-seeking behavior our emotional response is likely to be one of annoyance.[4]

Behaviors which suggest that power is the motive for the misbehavior are challenging disagreement, refusal to perform tasks or obey rules, questioning our judgement, invitations to "make me," doing just enough, or showing resentful compliance. When encountering these behaviors our response is likely anger.[5] There is an implied sense that our authority is being questioned.

Behaviors that suggest revenge is the goal of the misbehavior are name calling, leaving nasty notes, inviting you and other employees or superiors to fight, starting rumors, playing one-up by pointing out simple mistakes, especially in front of a group, signifying or talking about someone without calling their name (although loud enough for them to hear), explosive outbursts, sabotaging work, stealing, breaking equipment, or lying. We often respond to revenge behavior by feeling hurt.[6] When feeling hurt we often want to get even.[7]

Behaviors that would indicate a display of inadequacy as the motive for the misbehavior are: cutting work assignments, being a wallflower, acting-out to avoid embarrassment by storming out of the room, listing their own inabilities, trying something in order to prove that they can't do it, and showing illogical blame. The position of display of inadequacy can best be understood as an attempt to avoid criticism. When we encounter these folks we will likely feel despair or hopelessness.[8] Our most likely response will be wanting to give up or stop believing that the person can do anything right.[9]

Alternatives to our common responses are listed in the back of this book, as well as throughout the book. It is important to know what we are being asked because the different strategies are not always interchangeable. One of our bet keys is how we are feeling.

The reason for any behavior may be a combination of one or more of the four. For instance, in the letter excerpted earlier the woman was seeking to accomplish all four of the motives described. However, the good news is that we can choose which behavior and the ways that we will respond. We are not limited to the common reaction.

The following encounter illustrates one such choice. One inmate who was abused as a child did all of the following during an hour and a half group thereapy session with me. Twice she was distracting to the rest of the group. She reminded the group of my past mistakes. She spoke inappropriately and made funny remarks. She took charge of the group and asked flippant questions. Again, during a serious time she made jokes and was flippant. She used her tone of voice in a little girl manner, poked jest at the seriousness of the work that another group member was doing, and made a joke at my expense. She also made rude comments and directly put me down. This woman, described above, had few friends and had little ability to receive positive attention. At the time these remarks were made, she was hurting because her family ignored her.

In my response to her, I reasoned that all four of the goals for misbehavior were at issue. Revenge behavior implies a certain degree of hurt. It is those hurt feelings that I addressed and in doing so was able to provide her self-value, independent of her family's rejection. The methods of dealing with this situation is discussed in later chapters. However, of course, her behavior was addressed, and my response was chosen to protect the entire group, as well as to be effective with her. See if you can formulate a method of handling this woman. Begin with how you believe you would be feeling in the room with her as your key.

Occasionally verbal abuse, such as biting sarcasm or scorn, is used to elevate social status in the prison. The aggressor's position is enhanced in part because others don't want to be spoken to in a similar fashion. It becomes an indirect method of attaining leadership. When this is applied to gain control it is intermixed with moments of caring for the victim of the abuse. Physical threats or violence serve to enhance the effect.

All of these methods of gaining status through an indirect means of intimidation imply that gaining status through direct and honest means is a hopeless gesture. The anger openly directed toward authority figures may imply a minimal hope. Inmates who have been in the system for a long time tend to use this type of intimidation primarily on other inmates.

Direct confrontation is more likely to come from a person belonging to a minority group, while indirectly implying that an officer has made a mistake is more likely to be used as a means of control by white prisoners.[10]

How the person talks can be a key to what the person is expecting from us. There are four primary ways that persons who lived with much discounting respond to a threat in their environment. These are by becoming a placator, blamer, computer, or distractor.[11]

Essentially, placators do not believe that they can handle anger from others and often feel powerless.[12] They seem to want us to take care of them because of their feelings of helplessness. They are ready to please, willing to agree with anyone and any criticism.[13] These people never disagree.[14] Their behavior is manipulative because it does not take responsibility for the disagreements that are encountered. Placators want others to take care of their feelings without asking for that. Placators are generally very nice to our face, but will inadvertently get us. They will do this in a way that we will not easily be able to blame. Protecting ourselves ultimately with these folks means not letting them handle anything that is crucial. They have a habit of being where accidents happen to other people's stuff. For instance, my rug was stained, and my favorite cup broken; you get the idea.

The blamer wants others to believe that they are strong.[15] They find fault and feel lonely and unsuccessful.[16] People who blame others to avoid criticism must feel a great deal of guilt and responsibility, but they seldom voice their feelings of inadequacy, guilt, or responsibility. Their level of blaming will go up as any responsibility is attributed to them. They do not seem to know how to elicit nurturing responses from others, nor do they seem to know how to protect themselves when they are scared, except through blaming others.

The person who becomes like a computer feels vulnerable. They act mechanical and unruffled by happenings around them. The more scared they are, the more of a computer they become, making emotionless sentences. People who adopt the computer stance of avoidance seem to be afraid of any emotional display. They do not seem to know how to show or be shown affection. Their answer to life's difficulties is to become more logical. These people are often depressed and have encountered great loss in their lives which they have walled off by becoming more mechanical. To criticize a person using the computer stance will elicit a more mechanical response from them.

The distracting person doesn't believe that they have a place.[18] They make irrelevant comments, often responding to others by changing the subject either subtly or blatantly.[19] These folks flee criticism from others, often because they are highly self-critical and frequently carry a great deal of hurt. To criticize a distractor brings more distraction.

The four above methods or stances to the world all avoid being specific or making direct communication with their entire person. Being specific and communicating in a covert fashion usually brings negative responses. Since, what the person was trying to avoid was negative responses, they will be even more likely to repeat the same pattern. It doesn't matter that the patterned response doesn't work; it at least provides some feeling of protection.

Whether a person uses the distractor, computer, blamer, or placator role to avoid the feared from happening or experiencing it if it does, they are also hurting. The person using these methods knows that they do not work as well as they would like. They grew up using these methods to protect themselves and they are not going to change easily. Each of the four roles, point to a dysfunctional family; one that avoids certain topics or fears them being discussed. Each stance discounts the person using the position to cope with life. For instance, the distractor is implying that he cannot manage or deal with criticism. The blamer implies that he cannot accept any more responsibility. The placator avoids others arguing and thus implies that he cannot deal with two people whom he likes fighting or arguing. The computer doesn't believe that he can manage feelings. Each is afraid and becomes controlled by his fear.

The family that these people come from won't be made up of four distractors or four placators, but will have a variety of positions taken. Someone who placates may also switch to blaming or computing, and vice versa. As adults away from their family of origin they will surround themselves with people who will continue the same patterns. The family of origin will get re-created in the prison by the roles taken by others. In other words, if my mother was a blamer/placator and my father a computer, while I tended to shift from distractor to blamer, I will surround myself with people who also take these same roles. I may or may not view the person using the same role as a parent in the same way as my parent. However, I will find a way to re-create the dysfunction I grew up with.

Each of the four patterns of relating are communicating while denying the messages that are being communicated. If you ask blamers if they feel responsibility, they will tell you no! The distractor may criticize you in between subjects being changed and deny doing anything other than caring about you. The computer may say something that cuts to the quick and deny being angry at all. They are merely being logical, they would say.

One of the most frustrating ways of being conned is to have a person say something and then also have them deny that they have said anything. There are four areas of communication that can be denied. We can deny (1) that we have said anything, (2) that anything was communicated, (3) that it was communicated to a particular person, (4) the context in which it was communicated.[20]

Inmates frequently deny that they are communicating something when they tell us the words of another inmate who doesn't like us. By doing so they can deny feeling or thinking what they are attributing to the other person. This is a very angry gesture whether the inmate is aware of the effect or not. Consider the dilemma. We are told how an inmate doesn't like us and was calling us names in front of several others. However, we are being told about an inmate whom we thought liked us. There is no way to win in this situation. If we go to the third inmate we are going to get a denial. If we don't go to the third inmate we will be aware of the words said and wonder when we see the person.

More fights and arguments start over this type of thing happening between inmates than any other phenomena. Called "He say, She say" by the inmates, it is what keeps old arguments stirred and new ones going. Inmates new to the system tend to get caught up in the gossip of the prison and fall for this more than experienced inmates. In fact, if this is done to an employee by an experienced inmate, the chances are that it was thought out. If by an inexperienced inmate it is more likely that their anger may or may not be directed toward us.

Inmates deny that something was communicated by simply forgetting what they said, or by playing off their words as joking, or by excusing their body movements that indicated a message. I met one woman who could give you the blame for something in one sentence and two sentences later, if you asked her, couldn't remember ever blaming you for anything. If you had the impoliteness to question her further she would play it off, make a joke, and shoot at you two or three more times by saying something like, "How come you are picking on me? It's not my fault that you are so sensitive that you hear criticism everywhere."

When denying that a particular message was communicated, inmates will frequently do so by attacking the message. They can do this by attacking the logic, the scene, or the sequence of the events. Often the illogical rambling of their explanation takes us so far afield that we are less sure of what we first approached the inmate with in the first place. Eventually, it is obvious that the inmate isn't going to admit that a particular message was communicated. Persistence will only invite the inmate to get us behind our back. This ploy tends to be used more by very experienced inmates, people who grew up in the system. There is a certain artistic flair to this type of manipulative gesture. It will be combined with ramblings about how "You know that I wouldn't do that sort of thing."

When the context is denied, outside factors will become a factor, whether logical or not. Blame can be attributed quickly to fate, innocent bystanders, or coincidence. One of the more bizarre ways that the context of an inmate's behavior was denied occurred when a woman was asked about her case in which another woman was killed. She said, "It wasn't my fault, she (the woman killed) was just too tall. Had she been shorter she wouldn't have been shot."

No matter how a person talks with us, whether in angry tones or pleading ones, it is likely that they will be eliciting or seeking to elicit the very same type of interactions and attention, whether negative or positive, as they received as a child.[21]

How we are feeling can be a key to what a person is wanting from us or expecting from us, and can indicate the way in which they customarily responded to others. Our feelings and intuition are important indicators of what is happening between the inmates and ourselves. As noted earlier, when we are feeling annoyed, it is likely that the inmate is seeking to gain attention.[22] When we feel angry it is likely that they are seeking to control us.[23] When hurt, the possibility is great that the intent is to extract revenge. When we are feeling hopeless it is likely that the inmate's behavior is displaying inadequacy and avoiding criticism through their powerlessness.[24]

Blame that inmates attribute to us may be subtle and interlaced with half-hearted praise. Thus, if we are feeling guilty and we are not aware of what we have done, we may be with someone who wants control over our behavior and wants to extract revenge. One inmate at KCIW was almost infamous for her ability to manipulate staff's feelings by producing guilt with her subtle mixture of praise and implied blame. Anytime she was confronted with her implied statements, she would deny them vigorously, using one or more of the methods for denying communicated messages.

Occasionally, we experience fear inside prisons. No matter how often we tell ourselves that we don't feel fear, we do. Granted, for experienced officers it happens only on rare occasions, but it happens. Perhaps, the fear will be through our being intimidated. At times, with the most intimidating inmates, I have been shocked by the enormous amount of fear and hurt they covered by their angry mask. Inmates who use intimidation to coerce others are often the most fearful underneath their air of fierceness. Sometimes even more surprising is their sensitivity to others' pain, which they hide from themselves as well as others by forcing themselves to do what they are afraid of doing. Most actors need to feel the emotion that they are projecting. In other words, when we feel fear it is a good bet that the person we are afraid of is also afraid.

Dealing with sexual come-ons and subtle seduction in prison is a major problem area of manipulation, because even if we are not seduced, we can be had. In fact, the come-on may have nothing to do with sex. Sex may be the means for expressing the message. Because of this, employees whose only offense is not knowing how to respond to the unspoken message in seductive behaviors get fired, disciplined, and used. Obviously, some get fired because they acted-out; not because they were innocent.

Sex may be the means that anger, fear, revenge, or the desire for power gets channeled. Just because it might not be clear in the beginning that anger was the overall purpose in a seductive gesture doesn't make it any less so. Most institutions have experienced inmates who used sex to get people to leave them alone. At KCIW a woman mooned people, urinated on herself, would strip completely, and if none of those would work, she might masturbate. Few people would stick around to watch this 350 pound plus woman do many of these things. From the inmates she usually got laughter, but she was not ignored as she sometimes felt. Probably more than one reason may be applied to the woman's intentions. However, you get the point that sex may be used to communicate far more than sexual desire.

Consider the following scenario. An inmate with whom Officer Green has frequent dealings has become gradually more friendly and has been dressing more suggestively each time Officer Green is scheduled. Officer Green is aware of the subtle, increasing frequency of the seductive gestures by the inmate, yet does nothing, even though the other inmates are aware of these things occurring. Officer Green has already been had. If the officer says anything direct now, the inmate can complain that the officer is angry because the inmate stopped letting the officer have sex. It doesn't matter whether the person is the same sex or attractive or not, at this point, Officer Green has a problem. It doesn't even matter if Green is innocent, he/she has just lost.

While this scenario happened because of not speaking up, consider what would have happened if Green had labeled the behavior as seductive. The inmate could have become angry and made sure that everyone knew that Officer Green was trying to be seductive and had a perverted mind by thinking that everything was seductive when it was really innocent. The inmate could have easily exaggerated Officer Green's involvement. Green made a similar mistake by not addressing the unspoken message of the inmate's behavior from the first. Whether Officer Green enjoyed or disliked the inmate's seductive behavior, the inmate was in control.

We all know that words, phrases, and gestures can have more than one meaning. If one meaning is attributed, then another meaning can be claimed. However, if no blame is verbally attributed but only implied, then there is little that the inmate can use to try crucifying us with. For instance, while leading group counseling with a seductive woman who might allow her dress to open, generally will receive some variation of the following response. I ask to change chairs with the person next to the seductive woman. Someone may ask how come I have changed chairs.

My response will be so that I might be more of a gentleman since the woman next to me is wearing a distracting skirt. On the surface I have blamed her for nothing. However, during the entire group session she must sit there knowing that I have no intention of being maneuvered by her sexual behavior. The message is given to the entire group that I am about business.

No matter the setting or the message given with the seductive behavior, the way to counteract it is through the ulterior message given back. Ideally we want to give the impression that we are not scared or intimidated by the behavior. Recently in an office I saw the following sign that captures the essence of this type of intervention: "Sexual harassment will not be reported. However, it will be graded." The sign implies a number of things that all suggest strength not weakness.

Most of the obvious behaviors are easier to deal with, or spot. Things like progressive touching from inadvertent to less accidental looking, to the more blatant sexual come-ons or behaviors. These more obvious displays can be managed if the means is through the ulterior message given in return. However, the more subtle eroticisms of encounters are more difficult to manage, because there won't be specific behaviors to deal with.

Sometimes the best indicator is your own feelings. If you generally become aware of sex in a particular person's presence, they may be sexualizing the relationship. It may be happening through subtle movements that are out of your or the other person's awareness. Of course, it may be your own fantasy life, but barring that, it may be the person you are with, or the reality of the inmate's attractiveness. In any event it is wise to discuss the event with a coworker to enable you to de-escalate the effect by not keeping the encounter a secret. Talking with someone else will enable you to break the spell. It also is a safe thing to do because it says that you are a professional and are willing to be human although not manipulated by your humanness.

In discovering what is being expected of us, it is important to recognize the underlying meaning of behaviors, whether those are sexual or not. One way to discern is by the way we are feeling. However, if our customary response is something that everyone else would say in the situation, it might not be the most effective. For instance, if the customary response is one of criticism or anger, is it likely that when the inmate hears our angry criticism that they will hear it with any more impact than any of the hundreds of times in the past? As we saw earlier, people tend to seek attention, whether negative or positive, in the same way they did as children.[25] Our responding in an automatic way is generally neither helpful to ourselves nor the inmate. The inmate who is seeking a kick or criticism through misbehaving may stop misbehaving momentarily if corrected, but in the long run, this person will continue the pattern, and our predictable behavior simply reinforces the same old stuff.

While being yelled at is better than being ignored, there are other ways of getting attention. As an employee we may want to be more creative than to only respond with the predictable irritation or criticism. Sometimes doing exactly what isn't expected can have the most effective result.

One way to do this is illustrated by the following. A woman whom I will call Sheila attended group counseling and misbehaved in every conceivable way. She came late, became disruptive, acted out, made accusations, interrupted others, joked, etc. As I criticized her behavior or verbally noticed it, she would get quiet momentarily and then renew in some other fashion. I began responding to her with the words, "Sheila, you are really good at being bad," often smiling when I said the words. By commenting on her misbehavior in this manner, I was giving her a compliment, not criticism. However, her behavior was acknowledged. I might add that her misbehavior over a brief period ceased, and gradually she became the most productive and helpful member of the group. Did her behavior change simply because I refused to give her criticism and began pointing out behavior in a joking way? No. Sheila did find that in order to get attention from the group, she needed to begin behaving in other ways. Yet she was safe to change her behavior, because she sensed the group's and my real concern for her. By not criticizing her the way everyone else had, I avoided the power struggle that she invited and was able to win in the long run.

I like to believe that one reason Sheila was willing to hear something different was that I was speaking to an individual. Sometimes when we are commenting about a person's behavior we are not looking at the individual underneath the behavior. I think Sheila was willing to change in part because she liked being an individual rather than a misbehavior. Obviously, this happened in part by saying the opposite of what she was expecting.

I hope that it is unnecessary to say that speaking what isn't expected isn't always a responsible thing to do. Telling someone who is depressed and talking about suicide to go ahead is not only irresponsible, it is ridiculous. Yet, when we are saying the same thing that everyone else has told the inmate, how much power can we possibly expect from our words? In discovering what is expected from us, it is important to keep an open mind in that continuing discovery. Simply because we have discovered a pattern of relating only gives us clues about what is expected. Making a quick decision only invites our bad feelings and anger from the inmate.

When one women, Sherri, angrily refused to inform her volunteer visitor that she no longer wanted to have contact, I was confused at first. I reasoned that Sherri was not having difficulty asserting herself, because she was adamant with me. Fortunately, I was also aware that she was indigent and embarrassed to discuss her poverty. When Sherri understood that she was only being asked to inform the volunteer of her feelings and that postage would be taken care of by the institution, her attitude changed completely. Her lack of money was not discussed. It is often difficult for us to recognize that inmates sometimes do not have the price of a stamp and will go to great lengths at times to protect that secret. Sherri was willing to have gone to the cell block to protect her pride.

Even when we are certain of having discovered what is expected of us, it still shows wisdom to be slow in giving any advice. By giving direction or advice, we remove their possibility of feeling good about themselves and we set ourselves up. Problem solving does not involve our taking responsibility for the inmate. Advice is routinely rejected, because it does not respect the other person to think for him/herself. We tend to give it, because we feel better about ourselves when we have shown how intelligent and creative we are. We also set ourselves up and are not as intelligent as we would like to think when we disregard the consequences for the other person.

SUMMARY

In this section we reviewed four reasons for misbehavior which are: attention, power, revenge, and display of inadequacy. We described how it was important to understand the historical or current use of manipulative/disruptive behaviors. We also saw how generalized fears may inhibit a person's options. We discussed common manipulative phrases and words. We also saw how implied messages in conversations may be transmitted through both words and actions. We reviewed some methods of countering the implied messages and recognized that manipulation typically follows some real or synthetic intimacy. We also covered the manner in which sexual manipulation is generally done and means of deflecting its consequences. Finally, we saw that the underlying reason for manipulation is that a person is trying to do two things at once and is not giving full support to either or is denying both ulterior intentions.

In the next chapter we will see how discovering what is expected of us leads directly to the ways that the manipulator is not taking responsibility.

NOTES

[1] George F. Bennett, *When They Ask for Bread* (Atlanta: John Knox Press, 1978), p. 14.
[2] Ibid., p. 14.
[3] Don Dinkmeyer and Gary D. McKay, *Systematic Training for Effective Parenting: Parents' Handbook* (Circle Pines, MN: American Guidance Service, 1976), pp. 8-10.
[4] Ibid., p. 14.
[5] Dinkmeyer, p. 14.
[6] Ibid., p. 14.
[7] Ibid., p. 14.
[8] Ibid., p. 14.
[9] Ibid., p. 14.
[10] Lee H. Bowker, *Prison Victimization* (New York: Elsevier, 1980), p. 138.
[11] Virginia Satir, *People Making* (California: Science and Behavior Books, 1972), p. 63.
[12] Ibid., p. 64.
[13] Ibid., p. 63.
[14] Ibid., p. 64.
[15] Ibid., p. 63.
[16] Ibid., p. 66.
[17] Ibid., p. 68.
[18] Satir, p. 70.
[19] Ibid., p. 70.
[20] Jay Haley, *Strategies of Psychotherapy* (New York: Grune and Stratton, 1963), p. 89.
[21] Dinkmeyer, p. 14.
[22] Ibid., p. 14.
[23] Ibid., p. 14.
[24] Morris L. Haimowitz and Natalie R. Haimowitz, *Suffering is Optional: The Myth of the Innocent Bystander* (Illinois: Haimowoods Press, 1976), p. 4.
[25] Ibid., p. 4.

Chapter 3

DISCOVERING WAYS THE MANIPULATOR IS NOT TAKING RESPONSIBILITY

DISCOVERING THE WAYS the manipulator is not taking responsibility can be fun and rewarding, or it can lead to judgmental and critical attitudes that are frustrating and demoralizing. The choice is ours. Discovering the ways a person does not take responsibility is much like detective work and calls for intuition and judgment calls. Those judgment calls may lead to a critical list. It is easy to be critical of someone who is doing something and is so obviously manipulative. We can even be proud of the way we told them off, or pointed out what was wrong with them, or what was wrong with what they were doing. It is easy to become angry when we recognize an ineffective ploy to avoid work or guilt.

One of the times I became the most angry with an inmate was when she told me a sad story of how she had to steal in order to feed her children. When I checked her file, I realized that she was twenty-six and had never been gainfully employed. I was on the verge of being irrationally angry with the woman and thought how dare she excuse her behavior with such a flimsy excuse. I had worked since I was 14 doing all types of jobs that I didn't like. My anger with her taught me a lot about my own values. It said a lot about me, but very little about the inmate.

The Bible teaches us that overworking and irresponsible behavior to avoid life's difficulties are both sinful in the eyes of God. Our anger can teach us a lot about ourselves. Mine told me that I had just as much of a problem with working as the inmate did with not working. As I examined myself, I began to have more freedom to relate with the inmate in a different, more effective way.

It is important when we are discovering ways in which another person is not taking responsibility that we recognize the ways in which they discount us by their obvious ploys to avoid guilt or responsibility. Yet, these same ways in which we are discounted by the inmate are also implied to the inmate in her/his own words. Discounts go both to receiver and sender.

One question to ask ourselves is, "How is this useful?" Is it simply a matter of convenience, a learned response, a method of getting one up? We can also wonder if the manipulation is one that comes from a life-time of believed necessity of avoiding guilt of blame.

Abusive families are notorious for blaming each other and for their ability to avoid blame. Children growing up in such an environment learn quickly to shift blame. It comes almost naturally and spontaneously. They are also very keen about detecting or believing that others are still trying to pin things on them. In many cases they have given up, believing that they will be blamed whether they have done anything or not. Granted, inmates give plenty of reasons to be criticized. Imagine, if you will, growing up being blamed for things you couldn't possibly have changed, like your father's alcohol abuse, or his moodiness from his alcoholism. Perhaps, you simply felt shame because your family was poor, in trouble, or had a family member get ill or commit suicide. Fairly soon you might decide that whatever you did would be criticized and you might give up trying to do anything except what people expected. People who gain a measure of self-esteem from manipulative ploys have often encountered great losses and are not only fearful of further losses, but are fearful in general because of their state of anxiety that the first loss produced. Sometimes these people are mistakenly labeled antisocial, because they don't appear to feel guilt over their actions. If you already feel a ton of blame you might not notice another pound.

Fear is a powerful motivator. The military has long known this. Without new recruits being more afraid of their first sergeant and their platoon's reaction to their behavior, they just might not charge the enemy. Fear is something that is always with us. The determining factor is of what are we afraid? Fear is used in *The Bible* to refer to belief or faith, "The beginning of wisdom is fear of the Lord."[1] In other words, what we are afraid of, we have faith in happening. In fact, what we are afraid of happening we often unconsciously bring about through our fear.

Many inmates are very uneducated and have generalized fears, not only from their upbringing, but from the environment and changes they have undergone in being incarcerated. However, it is easy for the specific fear of being caught to become generalized into a fear of being detected, known, or understood. This is especially true of people who have been afraid of outsiders knowing about shameful events that occurred in their family of origin. In other words, if I am afraid that people will reject me if they knew that my father, brother, uncle, aunt, whoever had abused me, I will be likely to do things that people will reject me for. Furthermore, I won't be likely to want people to know much about me, because they might find out the secret that I fear people knowing.

It can be clear from the above that people often avoid responsibility, because they have taken on too much. The ways they avoid it in the present will be reminiscent of the ways that have been used historically. There will probably be patterned ways that responsibility is avoided. Once we detect the means in which it is done, we have a fair idea of how it will be in the future.

The way an inmate is not taking responsibility may be seen more readily from having detected what is expected of us. For instance, the person seeking power from us may be discounting his/her own abilities. He often believes that he is somehow incapable of receiving positive attention. These persons seldom believe that they have the right to make their own decisions and have those decisions respected and disagreed with at the same time.

People who have been abused as children and/or as adults are reluctant to trust, or they trust too much. However, most seem very reluctant to believe positive statements made about them. They also seem to believe that if they ask for something, it is of less value than if it were given without request. For example, many believe that if they have to ask for a compliment, it is of less value than if it were given spontaneously. With beliefs such as these it is easy to understand how it is important to manipulate others into giving what is wanted and deserved, yet not believed to be open for request. This makes receiving positive attention very difficult and calls into question the person's power and leaves him/her more prone to become angry. It is interesting that these same people do not act as if they have been complimented or noticed unless the attention was angrily or critically given.

When a person is avoiding or expecting to extract some measure of revenge, often what is being avoided is her/his own hurt feelings that lead to the desire for revenge. Think back on the times when you have wanted revenge. Wasn't the length of your desire for revenge closely related to how long you were still hurting? Even though we know that it won't take away from our pain, we still want some degree of satisfaction. What is being avoided is taking care of our hurt feelings and often even acknowledging that we are hurt.

In the previous chapter the difficulties of being unspecific were discussed. The language that is used often reflects what is being avoided. Some common phrases heard by people in corrections are, "You wouldn't understand," which translates to, "You wouldn't understand because you haven't been poor, black, a drug addict, prostitute, or homosexual." It implies that you are not smart enough or do not have the background to understand what would be told to you. The phrase also discounts the person's ability to explain to us what her/his experience was like. Another common phrase is, "I caught a charge" or "I caught this charge. . . ." which is said in the same manner that people talk about catching a cold, implying no responsibility for the actions leading up to being convicted. The phrase, "You know what I mean," is often used innocently enough by all sorts of people; however, the phrase can be used by manipulative persons to cover up the fact that they are not stating clearly what they mean.

When the above is said by a highly manipulative person, his/her attitude can also imply, "If I have to explain myself more clearly, then you are not as hip or likeable as I thought." If the person is being straightforward and simply frustrated, for the lack of adequate words, our requesting more information or seeking to clarify will be appreciated. The manipulative person may not appreciate our requests for clarity.

Probably the most common phrase heard in corrections is, "I don't know." This versatile and "catch all" phrase can be used to disguise anger, lie, excuse behavior, and express genuine lack of knowledge. It can disguise anger by being repeated when an answer is expected or wanted. Realize how angry we can become when repeatedly told by someone that they don't know. People use it to lie by not telling what they could. As an excuse, it can also imply guilt to a second or third party. Thus, someone should have told them. Its close relative, "Nobody told me," more clearly shows both the excuse and the implied blame. People using this phrase to manipulate are often seeking to cover their own guilt and personal sense of wrongdoing. "I don't know," used to convey lack of knowledge, is self explanatory. However, it is easily mistaken for the manipulative types of "I don't know." Possibly because we like telling others what we know, we get a good feeling from demonstrating how smart we are, and therefore we are easy targets. When we respond to the "I don't know" with information, it is likely that we have been had.

Another subtle way of controlling the person being spoken to is to change a want or desire to a need. The inmate simply talks about something that is wanted or desired in words that express need. When we think of need, we think of survival. Yet, when we think of a want or desire, we think of luxury. Inmates rarely think of this consciously, although they commonly change a desire to a need, and needs take on a different emotional value. While talking with someone who has confused the two we can easily be induced to think along the same path. However, subtly changing the label of need to want as we talk with the inmate can also have an impact on the genuine or sincere person. The out-and-out manipulator won't appreciate the subtle change that we introduce, and may become angry and say something like, "I should have known that you wouldn't understand. I guess you are like all the rest of the staff." Here the emphasis has now changed from responsibility the inmate was avoiding to the blame the staff is receiving.

Three words that are commonly used by inmates in manipulative fashions are *try, can't, and but*.[2] Although these words have legitimate meanings in the English language, they also are used illegitimately to avoid taking responsibility for what is communicated. The word "try" simply means fail. To say that we are going to try to dig a hole means that we will fail. One way to react or respond to the word try is to acknowledge the probable failure. For instance,

Inmate: I tried to stay clean this time.
Response: What does it feel like for you to know that you failed.[3]

"Try," used in the above, gives an excuse even before the attempt is made.

When used to express our ability, the word "can't" frequently means won't. Our mothers frequently told many of us that "Can't never did anything." Phrases like, "I can't understand how to forgive my parents, the warden, judge or whoever for what they did," translated means "I won't understand or forgive."[4] Unless it is a physical impossibility, most times can't means won't, but its use disguises the intent into an innocent one. That is how can I be guilty of not doing something if I can't do it.

The word "but" in the middle of a sentence negates either the first part of the sentence or the last part of the sentence, rendering the message unintelligible or rendering some part of the sentence meaningless. But, sometimes the word "but" is used without manipulation, of course. Some examples of the manipulative use of but are "I love you, but I really feel that I need to go out with some other people." Most of us have had that statement said to us at sometime in our life. Then when it was spoken to us, we knew quite clearly that the person saying it no longer wanted to be with us. "I would like to change, but I just don't think I can," translated means, "I won't change."[5]

Another way that the "but" is often used is to disagree without owning responsibility for that disagreement. When used like that it begins a sentence, and as such, discounts what the other speaker has said. In conversations in which many sentences are started with "but," both people are likely to begin feeling irritable and experience a certain degree of discomfort. When this goes on for any length of time without being addressed, it is likely that both people will go away with an unsatisfactory feeling about the conversation. A simple way to remedy this is to explain what the word "but" does to the meaning of a sentence, and ask the other person to disagree and be more open about his/her disagreement. It also helps us to indicate that we prefer disagreements to the "but." The use of the word "but" to begin a sentence frequently implies that the speaker does not believe that she/he can disagree openly. It means that the person believes that he/she must be covert in the disagreement. People commonly disagree with one another and they can have meaningful relationships irregardless of their disagreement. However, secretly disagreeing leads to a disruption in the relationship, because of the inherent dishonesty in the act. The average inmate does not use these words or phrases in a conscious effort to be manipulative. They are used because the inmate does not believe in his/her own abilities, or they have learned a bad verbal habit.

Manipulative common phrases that may or may not have conscious intent convey an implied message. The implied message may express contempt, by a way of getting revenge, or may be a way of exercising control over the hearer. A common way people joke around with one another illustrates this implied message. The phrase used in joking situations, "I don't care what everyone else says about you, I think you are an all right person."

The obvious implied message is that everyone else does not believe that you are OK. Implied messages are often disguised by giving others credit or blame for the statements. A few more examples follow: (a) "I recognize that you are really OK, and I just thought you ought to know that Vicki, the sergeant, the captain, etc., have been saying terrible things about you and maybe you ought to steer clear of them or straighten them out." (b) "You know that I like you, and how I feel about people talking behind other people's back. Well, you deserve to know that Sharon has been bad-mouthing you to everybody." The craftiness in this approach is that disagreement and dislike can be expressed to a person and blamed on the third party. Whether or not the speaker will accept responsibility for this type of angry gesture, or if the speaker is even conscious of the damaging nature is a moot question. Part of the hook is that this bit of information is told to us in confidence. Told to one person or officer about another officer's words can serve to disrupt the relationship between the two officers and embed the inmate in the first officer's good graces.

When we even listen or give acknowledgement to or encourage people to tell us what a third party has said about us, we invite ourselves to be manipulated. Protecting ourselves from this type of manipulation means being willing to forego hearing those juicy statements about ourselves. It also means giving up the feeling of being an insider with privileged information. It is tempting to want to hear what is being said about ourselves. However, once we have heard what this third party has said, we are left with only three choices: (1) confront them; (2) attempt to blot what was said out of our minds; or (3) deal with what was said inside ourselves.

Trying to blot out of our minds what a third party has said can sometimes be difficult, dependent on the hurtfulness of what was said to us. In either event, the inmate has won and we have been manipulated, if we allow ourselves to hear it. Even our allowing the inmate to tell us what she/he is trying to say suggests that we are easy. More disagreements, fights, and broken relationships are started at KCIW among inmates by this type of gossip than any other. In part, to confront the third party is to cast blame on them. The reasoning might go something like this: "What have I done that he doesn't believe in me any more than to believe that I would say. . . ." It implies that we do not trust them. Almost any way we might approach the third party implies that we doubted them, based upon what the first person said.

Unlike the implied anger in gossip, phrases like "nobody cares" imply that the person being spoken to does not care either. A phrase like "a real friend, fair person would . . ." implies to the hearer that if they want the speaker to continue thinking of them as "a real friend, fair person, etc., then they must do "X", "If he really loves me, he would . . . ." The above phrases spoken by themselves are easily discovered, it is when they are embedded within several other lines of information that they are more camouflouged.

Anyone who works in a correctional setting recognizes that there are two typical ways of verbally sending implied messages. One is by derogatory gossip, and the other is by the use of signifying. Inmates will often use derogatory gossip about an officer or another inmate to elevate her/his own self-esteem. The principle that is operating here is that if they are so bad, then I must be OK. Signifying, on the other hand, is speaking in a derogatory way about a third person who is present without addressing that person. A favorite is to do so in a mumbling voice that only allows some words to be caught by the person who is intended as the victim. The level and clarity become more understanable in a progressive manner that says how little respect the speaker has for the victim. A statement like, "Some officers here are so dumb, unfair, etc.," said to another inmate, can be covered, if questioned, by saying that the hearer wasn't being spoken to or about. "I wouldn't speak that way about you. You know that I tell people to their face what I say about them."

Frequently inmates will send implied messages by looks and stares. Over a period of time, an inmate may give sarcastic looks or make ugly faces and not respond when spoken to in a greeting by an officer. When this is done for a period of time by several inmates, the effect can be tiresome and irritating. The goal of such behavior may be to seek attention, provide revenge, attain power, derive satisfaction from the pleasure of inflicting pain, or to prevent their inadequacies from being known.

Some excellent wisdom about responding to these types of gestures is to never avenge ourselves.[6] To respond out of anger only lets the inmate know that we have been hurt. A response from our playful side implies that "I'm not bothered by your gestures." In fact, "I'll assume that you are speaking favorably to me, because I know that I'm OK." For example, in response to a mumbler, I might speak to the other person or persons in the room and say, "Gee, I could have sworn that someone was just complimenting me." "Were one of you saying something good about me?" The two guiding principles that I work from are (1) speak through the same line of communication, and (2) seek to be humorous. Even if we respond angrily, it is probably best if we utilize the same method of communication through the third person in the room. To not do so will invite a ridiculous disavowing of what was said.

One aspect of manipulation or intended control is that it usually comes after some degree of intimacy between people. Sophisticated inmates know that by being intimate with us and telling intimate aspects of their lives, we are more likely to reveal the same thing to them, or to grant special favors or privileges. New correctional employees are warned of this danger in corrections training. They are told that inmates schooled in street psychology know that a person extends liberties more easily to someone with whom they have shared feelings on a profound personal level, than when a person retains anonymity on such issues.[7]

One of the ways this synthetic intimacy is produced is by the "we/they" syndrome.[8] In this technique, the inmate refers to the officer and inmate as "we" and other officers, staff, etc., as "they." This creates a "we/they" situation that implies intimacy between inmate and staff member and an antagonistic position between "we" and "they." For example, an inmate might say to an officer while the institution is being cleaned for a special inspection and the officer is supervising the cleaning, "Hey, tell me how come we always have to put up with this stuff? They don't ever acknowledge the hard work we do; and they are the ones who get credit for the way the institution looks after inspection." The implied message is that the inmate and the officer are on the same level and "they," the administration, are against them or using them.

The above can seem trivial. It can appear that way because no one believes that such a simple statement can have much power. It doesn't by itself. It is the culminative effect of statements such as these that gradually erode the relationships between staff and build up an artificial relationship with inmates that can be exploited.

The reason that we want to discover the ways in which the manipulator is not taking responsibility is that it allows us to know the ways the person is stopping him/herself from achieving his/her legitimate goal, as well as alerting us to possible illegitimate goals. In the "we/they" example, if the intent is legitimate and the language is more habitual, then the inmate is putting him/herself down by believing that credit will somehow be taken from them, and not recognizing the worth of his/her own effort. In addition, if the legitimate intent is to foster a better relationship or merely comment on the similarities seen, then the inmate could use the information in a general sense that folks often resent in a appropriate inclusion, although they may not speak directly to the matter.

All of the ways that have been outlined or could be outlined in which one person manipulates another with intent to deceive for personal gain discount both people. Ordinarily, such devices are used when the person believes that she/he has no other means of achieving her/his goal. It matters little whether the goal is attention, power, revenge, or avoiding criticism. The more that we know about the way they are avoiding responsibility, the more that we can give that responsibility back with additional options for achieving goals.

For example, revenge or vindictive behavior is often used to elevate status.[9] Revenge is also used to decrease the amount of pain or hurt that the person is feeling. Giving inmates a more effective way of stopping the hurt also increases their options. It helps us and lowers the amount of tension an inmate feels. In the long run, it can help inmates to feel better about themselves. An incident that illustrates this came from a resident who was ready to fight, because other inmates had been teasing her and she didn't know anything else to do. As we talked, it became evident that she could feel better if she had another way of protecting herself from the hurtful things that other inmates were saying about her. When she recognized that she had some effective "come backs" to their teasing, she no longer was feeling hurt but proud of her new power. Learning new skills more often encourages most of us to feel better about ourselves.

A careful student of manipulation may notice that all the ways of avoiding responsibility have one similarity. They are attempting to do two things at the same time without taking responsibility for either of the two. It is one thing to do two things at the same time for efficiency's sake. It is downright self-destructive to attempt two things at the same time because we don't believe that we can do either successfully. The most common reason that a person does not achieve his/her goal is for being like the proverbial donkey between two bales of hay, deciding to go to neither hay bale and standing in the middle.

Before we on to giving responsibility back, one word of caution is in order. We can easily have misjudged or missed our guess about what the goal of the inmate's behavior is. The more we keep an open mind and remain searching for continuing clues, the more likely we are to be successful.

SUMMARY

We saw that our anger may teach us more about ourselves than the manipulator in this section. We also reviewed how discounts are implied in the relinquishing of responsibility. We covered how some of the reasons for this discounting of responsibility come from fear, historic abuse, and anxiety about being hurt or vulnerable.

In addition, we covered some typical phrases and words that are used to discount responsibility. We saw how angry messages are implied in third-party gossip and reviewed ways to stop the gossip. We also saw how anger is implied in need and in gossip that is not directed to us.

We also discussed alternative methods of dealing with people who try to hurt us and how hurtful methods are more likely to be used on us after some degree of intimacy has been established. Ways to produce a synthetic intimacy were illustrated. Finally, we examined the reasons for understanding and detecting the avoidance of responsibility.

NOTES

[1] *The Bible.*
[2] George F. Bennett, *When They Ask for Bread* (Atlanta: John Knox Press, 1978, pp. 43-45.
[3] Ibid., p. 43.
[4] Ibid., p. 42.
[5] Ibid., p. 44.
[6] *The Bible*, Romans 12:19.
[7] Office of Corrections Training Lesson Plan, "Human Relations, Staff/Inmate Relations," *Diagnosing Criminal Behavior*, 101100.000.000, p. 9.
[8] Ibid., p. 10.
[9] Lee H. Bowker, *Prison Victimization* (New York: Elsevier, 1980), p. 66.

Chapter 4

GIVING BACK RESPONSIBILITY

GIVING BACK RESPONSIBILITY is somewhat of an art, in that each person's unique style of doing so can be utilized. We want to find out what works best for each of us. One person's methods may be seen and felt as phony when imitated by another. In this section a number of options will be given to stimulate the readers' thinking. The most important thing, however, in returning responsibility is our attitude toward responsibility and inmates.

If we are wanting to pin something on an inmate or accuse them of behavior, or get them to acknowledge what they have done for our satisfaction, then none of these techniques will work. They may prove to be antagonistic. However, if we are willing to like the inmate in spite of her/his misbehavior and destructive manipulations, we have a plus on our side. Irvin Yalom in his now classic study about psychotherapy found that the most effective or curative factor that was listed by patients in his study was "discovering previously unknown positive factors about themselves."[1]

Almost anyone can find fault with another person, but finding the positive characteristics of that person takes a little more time and energy. As Yalom's study suggests, the time and energy can be well spent. The amount of responsibility that is returned and our style in returning that responsibility needs to match the type of inmate that we are dealing with.

Although each person and each inmate is a unique human being, I find it helpful to characterize inmates into one of four types. The types that are illustrated below are not meant to be all inclusive, nor are they meant to be the only way that we can think of inmates. I simply find that categorizing into types helps in deciding how to respond in a more effective and intentional way. Using types to describe people isn't new. In *The Bible*, Proverbs categorized the fool into different types.[2] Although our English Bibles do not reflect the difference, the Hebrew root words reflect descriptions that range from mentally deficient to openly antagonistic to God.[3] There is an intentional matching of the following categories and the Hebrew meanings. You will remember that the fool in Proverbs is someone who is not giving allegiance to God. That is, someone unconcerned about the First Commandment. In each case, the Hebrew meaning follows my label: (1) special needs—"inclines to a subhuman mentality, brutishness (basically retarded);" (2) regular folks doing time—"simple, largely through want of experience;" (3) loser—"is less innocent than the merely foolish;" (4) ultimate loser—"often appears to be an understatement for outright sinfulness."[4]

Special Needs

Inmates with special needs frequently are retarded emotionally, socially, or intellectually. They are people with chronic problems of attention needs. Staff members spend an inordinate amount of time working with them in proportion with the numbers of the population. These inmates frequently have poor work records and adjustment records. They are often teased, provoked, and harassed by other inmates, sometimes just for the fun of it and sometimes because they are different from other inmates.

One retarded woman who could be easily categorized as having special needs was a grossly overweight woman. She was very retarded and was harassed by inmates. She looked and talked different from the others. When she was harassed, she would often take off her clothes, make obscene gestures, and/or urinate on herself. On the street she was able to live only because of receiving disability payments. In fact, even in prison she was able to hold few jobs and spent most of her time in the cell block for disciplinary behavior. Because of her childlike quality, a number of people would talk down to her by using baby talk when speaking to her. When people did this, she responded very poorly. She may not have been very bright, but she knew when people were talking down to her. She could easily get on peoples' nerves by asking repeatedly the same question and it took patience to work with her. She liked me and would do most of what I asked her to do, simply because I treated her with respect and answered her questions, even when it felt like she had asked the same question seventy times seven times.

Losers

This group is characterized by having a long history of one disastrous mishap after another. One woman who is representative of this group at KCIW had the "midas" touch in reverse. She had gotten her life into such a mess that three people constantly planning probably couldn't have created such a mess. Weldon Fuller, a former chaplain at KCIW, found that women he tested had "loser scripts."[5] Fuller states, "They have stroking patterns that are more negative in terms of intensity and frequency."[6] People whom I think of in terms of loser identities do not seem to have the ability or knowledge of methods to give and receive positive strokes toward other people. They usually receive attention or acknowledgment of their existence only through their misdeeds. They are very susceptible to criticism, because they do not feel good about themselves.[7] Losers get into lots of trouble and receive disciplinary write-ups. Their goals are seldom met, and often their goals for the future are unrealistically high. Losers are seldom able to plan some sophisticated con, but are the ones who get involved in carrying it out and are the ones who get caught. In my thinking, the majority of the population of state-run correctional facilities could be considered or typed as losers. Their charges are often so blatant that when reading the police reports, one wonders if they were wanting to get caught. Their family histories are disaster stories of abandonment, abuse, and tragedy.

Ultimate Losers

The ultimate loser in my mind is the antisocial personality. *DSM III: Diagnostic and Statistical Manual of Mental Disorders* describes them as having "a history of continuous and chronic antisocial behavior in which the rights of others are violated. . . ."[8] Their behavior is further elaborated by the following: "lying, stealing, fighting, truancy, and resisting authority are typical early childhood signs."[9] Inmate files seldom, if ever, record this type of childhood information. However, inmate files do contain data both directly and indirectly that suggests the behaviors listed as typical of adolescence. ". . . usually early or aggressive sexual behavior, excessive drinking, and illicit drugs are frequent."[10] The antisocial inmate's adult record will reveal a continuation of these adolescent trends, ". . . with the addition of inability to sustain consistent work performance or to function as a responsible parent and failure to accept social norms with respect to lawful behavior."[11]

These people have few friends, although other inmates will often be around them. They seem not to be able to stop conning, even when it is in their own best interest. These folks often want a lot of staff and volunteer contact. They accept little or no responsibility for their behavior and seem to have almost a flagrant disregard for the rights and privileges of other human beings. These people frequently use their criminal behavior or manipulations to compensate for their own low feelings of self-esteem.[12]

Folks evidencing the antisocial personality are often thought of as having a compulsive need to manipulate.[13] With this stance toward the world, it is small wonder why they would feel lonely and have few close friends, especially, since no one seems to be given immunity to their antics. In spite of their track record, they seem to be able to make favorable first impressions.[14] How else could they get a person's confidence in order to con them?

When we consider what their life amounts to and the relationships they trade for trinkets, how could they be considered to be anything but the ultimate loser? They make the famous trade of Manhattan for beads look like a good deal. They trade momentary feelings of superiority through their manipulations for a lifetime of distrust, bitterness, and loneliness.

Regular Folks Doing Time

Volunteers often give the impression that they believe that most of the inmates fit into this category. Staff members usually believe they make up the smallest percentage of the population incarcerated, if they exist at all. I believe they differ from the loser in that during their incarceration they cause little if any trouble. When these folks approach a staff member, it is usually for a straightforward request. They tend to manipulate in destructive ways very little. They do not seem to play the prison games. They appear to want only to do their time and to leave. They openly admit their mistakes and take full responsibility for their actions.

The tendency to enlarge this group, or to be quick to believe that a prisoner is in this group, probably accounts for more disappointment on the staff's and volunteer's part than any other single factor. It is not a simple matter of being able to determine who belongs in which category by sight. Yet, to treat the four groups the same is disastrous. The inmate with special needs cannot be expected to change overnight and requires special handling. That is not to say special treatment. The loser and the ultimate loser also cannot be treated the same when returning responsibility. For instance, losers will often be almost glad they were corrected, while the ultimate loser will strenuously deny and be almost convincing. Arguing with the ultimate loser is fruitless, while the loser will sometimes hear logic and respond. Proverbs tells us that we cannot win an argument with the ultimate loser, whether we are angry or good natured.[15]

One of the best ways to give responsibility back is to ask lots of questions. Asking questions can be confronting. I am reminded of a minister who was famous for confronting people during slavery times with the immorality of slavery. What he did was just ask people questions about slavery that got them thinking and questioning their behavior. Asking questions like who, what, where, and when helps the other person think through their own behavior.

One question that most of us are quick to want to ask is seldom of help. That question is why. From it we can receive clever explanations. We won't get answers.[16] Asking why is not helpful. The reaction that many people have to the question "why" is defensive. People often act like we have just implied guilt when we ask them "why." The question seems to imply that we disagree with or dislike what was said or done.

Ideally, our questions can also imply that the inmate also has abilities and that we believe in those abilities. Lots of therapists ask questions and refuse to give answers, because it helps the other person to develop their own resources.[17] Our refusal to answer questions about what another person should do can give them the impression that we believe in their ability to make good decisions. The opposite is also true. Telling others what they should do discredits their ability to make a good decision.

When we are giving back responsibility it is seldom helpful to simply say the same thing that everyone else has or would say. If what everyone else said was effective, then there would be no need to repeat it again. Most of us know how useful lecturing a child is in getting him/her to change his/her behavior. The average inmate has heard the same lectures and criticism repeatedly for years. It isn't likely that our lectures are going to be any different. I believe that we can tell people what we think for our own satisfaction and not for their benefit.

All of the following approaches or options for dealing with disruptive or manipulative-like behavior are things all of us do with people we care about. What is different is intentionally doing these things with people whose behavior and personality we don't enjoy. Many of the options may sound manipulative, and they are. Remember that *Webster's Dictionary* defines manipulation with two basic meanings, one as skillful handling and the other as deceptive control.[18] Furthermore, the following statements can also be true, if we allow them to be. They have also been chosen to imply ability to the inmate instead of criticism or distrust.

A few techniques or options for dealing with inmates whose goal is attention are the following: *We can reinforce the stopping of an annoying behavior and attribute a positive motivation to the communication that comes through the annoying behavior*. We do this by ignoring the disruptive behavior until the person has stopped and then comment positively on his/her stopping. For instance, an inmate who is tapping on the side of his bunk would be ignored until he stopped, and then would receive a thank you for stopping. When we *attribute a positive motivation* to his/her communication, we offer the inmate a face-saving way of maintaining the relationship. An example of this would be in the response to an inmate who continues to make cute comments. We might say, "It is flattering to think that you like me so much to make such comments." The inmate will, of course, deny liking us that well. In similar fashion as response to an inmate who repeatedly disagrees with us can be, "I didn't know that you felt so strongly about me, I like you, too." The inmate's response will be to deny liking us. Occasionally, the inmate will challenge our statement that we like them by asking what we like. Knowing what we like and not needing to search for words at this point makes us sound much more believable.

This approach gives back responsibility to the inmate for her/his need to get attention and states an obvious way the inmate can receive more positive attention, that is by telling others what he/she likes about them. In another subtle way, it points out the effectiveness of what they are doing to receive attention.

Planned ignoring means just that. We plan to ignore a particular attention-getting behavior, and thus refuse to give negative scolding for this attention seeking. It is a way of directing the inmate to stop by choosing not to reinforce it with our criticism.

Signal interference is an approach used by most parents and every teacher to get a child or student to stop his/her disruptive behavior. It simply means that we look at, give a stare, walk close to, or make some slight gesture to illustrate our disapproval. Similarly, *Proximity control* is an option in reducing attention-seeking behavior by walking close by the person being disruptive. These approaches are best when used along with others that reinforce and guide the inmate to seek attention through positive means.

Rechanneling is one of these methods for guiding the person to a more constructive behavior. My three-year-old son taught me this method by developing the obnoxious habit of banging his fork on the table. He soon showed me that fussing at him or criticizing his noisy banging worked for only a few seconds. He would then begin on the glass, plate, or anything handy. When I finally caught on, I started bringing with us to restaurants cars or small toy figures. When he would begin to drum beat, out would come a car and an invitation to play. He got the attention he wanted and he didn't make noise.

Another way along the same lines is to give excessive attention. Essentially, this is a combination of *rechanneling, reinforcing positive behavior*, and *proximity control* all at the same time. To use this option we simply give *excessive attention* and keep doing it until it is obvious that the inmate has been overloaded with the attention. At the same time, we don't say anything about the negative behavior. Asking the inmate to do a number of jobs that keeps her/him close to us is one way of applying this method. Only the slowest inmates fail to get both points that there are better ways of getting attention than by their disruption, and that we like them enough to have them close to us and to avoid embarrassing them by criticism.

Relabeling behavior as positive is more than changing labels for a product. It is also changing which product we choose to comment about. For instance, when an inmate seems to have the ability to ask all the questions that we will say "no" to, we have the option of commenting on his/her ability to get people to say "no" to them rather than saying "no" once again. For example, "You are really good at getting people to say 'no' to you." When the inmate persists in a number of small disruptions, he/she can be told, "You are really good at being bad." By relabeling his/her behavior in this positive light, we return responsibility without escalating or reinforcing the cycle of negative behavior by criticism. It also lets the inmate know that the answer is "no."

Occasionally, however, giving positive labeling or some type of positive compliment will not work. With some inmates accustomed to criticism as the only type of acknowledgement, we often need to give criticism with feeling and begin to use other methods or options in a more gradual way. Although giving criticism will not help in changing the disruptive behavior, it does suggest to the inmate that we care about them. When giving this type of criticism with feeling, if the inmate smiles or begins to act as if they have been praised, we can know that we guessed correctly.

Some approaches for dealing with inmates' misguided attempts to achieve power are the following: We can *secure cooperation on an unrelated task*. When we recognize that we have met with disagreement and they are simply going to refuse to cooperate on a particular task, we can often gain cooperation by offering another assignment, even one that is less desirable in our mind. This increases the likelihood of assistance on the first task as well as the second. Doing this does not diminish our authority, in fact, it might increase our authority. One occurrence that comes to mind happened one day in the chapel when a particular inmate was asked to buff the floor. The inmate had frequently been asked to do this task and was angry that she was being asked again. It became obvious that if she were pushed on the issue, she would be willing to receive a disciplinary write-up rather than lose face and buff the floor. She was given the option of cleaning the toilets or buffing the floor. She was very happy to clean the bathrooms and the toilets. This allowed her to save face, even though she may not have enjoyed the second option. Yet, it avoided a continuing power struggle. By *securing cooperation on the unrelated task*, we are at the same time withdrawing from the current power struggle and letting the inmate know that we are taking seriously his/her feelings. Rather than escalating the struggle into an offense that requires a write-up and calling attention to our need to enforce our authority by sheer force, we can maintain the relationship and allow both of us to win.

Agreeing to disagree suggests that the other person is taken seriously. It implies that the other person has the right to disagree as well. Agreeing to disagree sets the stage for using this technique with an inmate who does not feel the permission to disagree except through huge arguments and can be very freeing. If we need for an inmate to agree with us about everything, then we have more of a problem than they do.

Another option for dealing with power struggles is to *decontaminate through humor*. One way that I use this option in group therapy sessions occurs when several inmates are making statements that question my judgment. I might throw up my hands and say, "I think that all of you are taking potshots at me," and laugh. Using humor in this method comments on the unspoken behavior, yet refuses to argue or attempt to prove who is right. This option suggests that we are comfortable with both ourselves and others pushing us. It demonstrates our strength.

Offering choices is still another option. It is different from securing cooperation, because offering choices means that we are not concerned about the first task. If our goal is to get both tasks accomplished, then we are not wanting to give much of an option. Another option for dealing with power struggles is to admit our defeats, *own our responsibility in the difficulty, and ask for help*. For instance, when an inmate has refused to perform a task or obey a rule, we can admit that we cannot force them to work. We can accept our responsibility by stating that we still need to have the job done and ask them for their help in accomplishing the task. If the inmate chooses to help, she/he can attain a sense of power even though she/he has still done what we have asked. Their refusal may well have had nothing to do with us, but was the frustration they were feeling in the first place. Admitting defeat is often a very powerful thing to do. It implies that our ego is not out of hand.

Challenges to our power that do not require write-ups involve a different option. *Stroking the inmate's independence and requesting a negotiation* is a way of giving attention instead of criticism. When an inmate challenges our judgment, we can say, "I like the way you can come to your own conclusions and think for yourself. Let's negotiate a way that both of us can get what we want. I need these different jobs done. How can we work this out?" When we take this type of stand, we are suggesting that the inmate has a mind and is capable of using it, instead of protecting our need to know everything and inviting an escalation of a power struggle.

When it is very obvious that the inmate refuses to perform a task or when she/he is simply inviting a "showdown" by taking a "make me" attitute, we can comment on the obvious. That is, *identify the power struggle*. One example is "I really get uncomfortable when we get into this tug-of-war over whether or not you are going to do the jobs that are assigned to you." Occasionally, inmates get into power struggles when they are hurting the most. It becomes a way of attracting attention to the fact that they are hurting. Having heard bad news from home doesn't excuse their behavior. If we simply give them a write-up when they just heard that the courts are moving to terminate custody of their children, we will not have done anything toward future cooperation either. Noticing that they are more touchy on a particular day usually involves this option.

Still another option for blatant power struggles of this sort can involve *remembering more positive times*, like the following: "Hey, let's stop this tug-of-war for a second. Remember the time we sat outside and talked about your hope for the future? I felt close to you at that time and I would like for us to work together today like we did that day." In a sense, this type of maneuver involves a negotiation of sorts. It is trading attention for cooperation. The principle here is to remember a more positive time with the inmate, in order that he/she may choose to feel good about him/herself and get some emotional distance from the current struggle.

Rechanneling the desire for power is a way of avoiding a power struggle and at the same time seeking to gratify in part the inmate's need for attention and power. Given the same scenario as in the above with the inmate refusing to perform an assigned task, we can request information about why they are more irritable today. If they are frustrated because of some isolated issue, we can talk with them about their options. By problem solving with the resident, we would have made a friend. The very act of problem solving helps a person to become aware of his/her alternatives. Knowing alternatives is a means of power itself.

Interest boosting works in much the same way in that by increasing the person's interest in the task or in obeying a rule, they receive alternatives. Often an inmate's interest is low because they feel that no matter what they do it will still be wrong. Interest boosting being used with an inmate who is doing just enough to get by might be done by commenting on how good a job they are doing while the job is still being done. This is to be done instead of commenting at the end and pointing out how the job is not perfect. If their interest has been boasted by the compliment, it is more likely that cooperation will be secured for the full task. If the inmate feels like we are taking them seriously, their interest in working with us will be increased. Another reason that interest is low is that sometimes the inmate just doesn't understand how to accomplish the task. Breaking the job into smaller parts which are explained is a method of interest boosting.

Asking how to gain cooperation is still another means of implying to the residents that we take seriously their thoughts and feelings when they are refusing to perform tasks, etc. Asking for cooperation implies to the person that you do not have the power to force compliance and, in fact, you don't. Anyone who has tried to force a toddler to cooperate knows the futility of gaining cooperation by force. When we are actively engaged in a power struggle with an inmate who is questioning our judgment or refusing to perform a task, we are often feeling threatened. Clearly stating how we feel threatened suggests that we are willing to recognize the power struggle with the inmate who is questioning our judgment or refusing to perform a task. Clearly stating how we feel threatened suggests that we are willing to recognize the power of the person. Doing so can be part of securing cooporation, because it denies our being in a one-up position. On another level, stating that we feel threatened implies that we are secure in ourselves and our position, so secure in fact that we can be down right human.

Stating how we feel or exaggerating the way that we feel in a humorous way can also be a powerful means of dealing with power struggles. By exaggerating how we feel, we are acknowledging the power that the inmate does have as a human being. However, we are also implying that we are not so afraid of that power as to lose our sense of humor.

A method that I frequently have fun using is to request the behavior that is challenging or disruptive. For example, several women have found numerous ways to refuse to do what I have asked, especially in group therapy where many have more sense of freedom to be rebellious. I have often requested them to continue to be disruptive and to be even more creative in their choices. I pull out a piece of paper and pencil and begin writing down the options they come up with, thanking them for being so compliant in teaching me more ways of misbehaving. In this situation, no matter what the woman does, she must be compliant. If she continues to misbehave, she is only doing what I have requested. If she discontinues the misbehavior, then she is being compliant. I have allowed many inmates to teach me about being disruptive or challenging. This is not just a gimmick, I am serious about my willingness to learn from them. Often at the same time that I request the misbehavior, I may very well relabel it as positive.

The story of one woman, in particular, illustrates the effectiveness of the above method of relating. This woman would refuse to talk while she was in group and would be disruptive at times when others were talking. I both requested her behavior and relabeled it as positive including the avoidance of revealing anything about herself. I would say to her that she was good at being bad. I also explained to the group that she was one of those rare people who learned more by being quiet than by talking about herself. In a short while, she worked hard to prove that what I had said about her was true. In time, she became one of the most valuable group members in keeping the group on their task and in demonstrating how much she had changed. The unspoken message in using this strategy is that we like the person enough to see beyond her/his disruptive behavior.

Misbehavior or manipulative-like behavior that can be understood to have revenge as a goal can better be understood as a means to deal with an inmate's hurt. We want revenge because we are hurting, or at least we remember the hurt so well that we are still able to recall its presence. In other words, we want them to hurt because we hurt, and we want to hurt the other person usually as long as we are still hurting. Some of the most effective ways of dealing with revenge behavior are to speak to the *person's hurt and ignore our own for the moment*. However, it needs to be understood that if revenge behavior warrants disciplinary action, then it is our responsibility to provide that. Even so, our response to the inmate initially does not necessarily need to involve discussing the consequences of their behavior. For instance, with an inmate who gets caught stealing and who doesn't usually steal we might initially talk with him/her about the possible hurt feelings first. Often an inmate will steal something that he/she may or may not want when he/she is experiencing a particular pain in his/her life. One instance of this occurred when a woman went on a stealing spree from other residents, when she found out that her husband was starting court proceedings to terminate her custody of their child. Of course, her pain does not justify her behavior. Yet, not taking the opportunity to let her talk about her fear and hurt before she is informed that she will be written up avoids a good opportunity to help shape her behavior.

Although name calling can be revenge behavior, it can also have other motivations that are more manipulative like. We need to decide at the time what the motivation is in order to deal with it effectively. Being prepared with some ready comebacks is helpful. One that has worked for me is illustrated in the following. When an inmate, whom I will call Vicki, began calling me names in front of other inmates, I walked over to her, ignoring her name calling, and said to her, "You know, I like you, too, and I just want to thank you for having such strong feelings toward me." She, of course, challenged my liking her and asked me in a sarcastic voice what it was that I liked about her. I was prepared, knowing that she wouldn't believe me, and I specifically told her what I liked about her. She was speechless. The other inmates were impressed. I avoided a difficult situation and actually made a friend rather than an enemy. Neither Vicki nor the other inmates who were present have since called me names to my face.

Accepting strong feelings as a compliment is a way of stating what many inmates believe secretly anyway. A high percentage of the incarcerated have been abused as children, or have lived in abusive environments as children and/or adults. In these situations often the only attention they received was through yelling and bickering. I am particularly reminded of one inmate who was asked to recall some of the fond memories she had of the holidays when growing up. With a far-away look in her eyes, she said, "What I miss most about the holidays is being in the kitchen and yelling and arguing with everybody while dinner was being fixed." What was more shocking than her statement was that six or seven other inmates overheard her statement and none of them objected. Several even shared the kinds of things their families argued about.

When people begin playing one-up by pointing out simple mistakes in front of a group or using some other ploy, one way of responding is simply to *play one-down*. Commenting on or exaggerating our hurt, inability, and responsibility is another method.

Signifying is frequently used as a means of extracting revenge on other people, including staff. Signifying is talking about a person to a third party without naming or speaking directly to the second party.

Humorous derailment works well in responding to signifying. An illustration of this came from an inmate I will call Betty. She was distressed that other inmates were teasing her and using signifying remarks to hurt her. Their comments were successful when they began to tease her about a friendship she had implied — that she and her friend were lesbians. After we talked, she agreed to let me know how she handled the situation. The next time the other women began signifying about her being homosexual, she blew them a kiss and pranced out of the room. This approach leaves room for the first inmate to save face, because she can now act as if she were just kidding and not meaning to be hurtful.

If, in fact, we are willing to have revenge behavior repeated, we can *request the inmate to repeat the behavior*. When an inmate is pointing out our simple mistakes in front of other inmates, we can request that inmate to point out all of our simple mistakes and let the inmate know we appreciate her help. It is not often that we get someone to take that great an interest in what we do. Finally, in a more serious note, we can give power back to the inmate by asking him/her to resolve the dilemma with us. An inmate who is caught lying can be responded to by stating that we can't know what to do with the situation and ask the inmate how this dilemma could be resolved.

Again, I want to reemphasize that behavior which warrants a write-up needs to be documented, even though one or all of these methods are used before the write-up is completed. The key, I believe, is how we respond first to the inmate's behavior, rather than trying to clean up our relationship after we have issued a disciplinary report. The way in which we respond first gives a message whether we intend for it to or not. By first giving the write-up or talking about it, we have said without words that the rule is more important than the person. After this has been stated nonverbally, efforts to change the inmate's perception of the way we feel toward him/her will be of little value.

Some options for responding to displays of inadequacy are intended to speak to the underlying feeling of rejection or lack of hope the inmate has. Offering only criticism for displays of inadequacy only reinforces the inmate's belief that there is no hope for him/her to change. Displays of inadequacy such as cheating, acting out to avoid embarrassment, storming out of a room, lying about work that has not been done, not bothering to do work, can all be dealt with by some of the following methods.

We can *exaggerate our own inadequacies* in one or two ways, by either emphasizing our inadequacy to force the person to do the work, or by talking with the person about the things which we are unable to do. By stating the obvious that we cannot force them to work, we imply personal power to the inmate. When we exaggerate our own inadequacies in other areas, we imply indirectly that the inmate and ourselves are similar and if similar, there is hope for the inmate because we are capable in other areas.

Another way we can speak indirectly to the inmate's feeling of rejection or lack of hope is to *compliment any effort*. In essence, this is refusing to be critical of the work that is done. For instance, when inmates do not bother to do their work and their goal is to avoid the embarrassment of admitting they cannot do something, getting into a power struggle with them over whether they will complete the task or not is useless at best. Asking them what they have done or the ways they have attempted to do the task and complimenting sincerely any effort they have made is encouraging compliance. Sometimes distinguishing the inmate who is operating from a position of inadequacy is difficult to recognize from one who is simply into a power struggle. One of the reasons that recognition is so difficult is twofold. First, the inmate has a lot of practice in hiding his/her inadequacies, and secondly it is often out of our ordinary experience that another person is incapable of what we think are simple tasks. Recognize how just not being able to read can cripple a person from completing many simple tasks.

It is not unusual for special needs inmates to cover up their known inabilities. Many have spent a lifetime hiding the fact that they are unable to do jobs that many of us take for granted. Reducing the task to its simplest elements helps reduce some of the overwhelming nature of a complex set of directions. When an inmate, whom I will call Lucy, is told to clean the chapel, she usually will get angry. However, if she is told specifically what to do and not all at once, she often will do the work on her own. Lucy is very sensitive to remarks she believes are discounting, criticism or a put down. She has gone to great lengths to avoid situations where she feels incompetent. On many occasions she has been willing and ready to go to the cell block rather than admit her feelings of inability.

Another inmate, whom I will call Anna, taught me how important it is to know the capabilities of the people with whom we are working. Anna had learned ways of responding to questions which allowed others to believe that she was bright, capable and aware of what others said to her. When I became puzzled about Anna's lack of customary responses to things I said to her, I checked her file and asked a staff member who knew her well. The staff member's response was, "Anna is the only inmate who I am afraid will get lost between the dining room and the dorm." The staff's comments were not cruel. The woman I'm calling Anna had a very limited intellectual capacity, even though she could superficially give people a false impression of herself.

How can we tell if we are dealing with a display of inadequacy or with someone extracting revenge or power? Often during the exchange we cannot. It is only by observation and verification of ability either from other staff or from the inmate's file.

One method of reducing anxiety in an inmate who has given up on herself or changing her life is by *requesting failure*. Sincerely requesting failure of a particular job or attaining some measure of excellence is a way of saying that we accept the person whether he/she is successful or not. Requesting failure is a means of continuing a relationship, because it implies that we are going to remain a friend no matter what the inmate accomplishes. When using this option, we must be careful to avoid sounding as if we are belittling the other person.

A variation of the above is to *respond to the inmate's success with surprise*. This increases the likelihood that the inmate will recognize that she/he has done something right. The reason is that their success was not predicted, thus they can recognize that some of the people who have predicted their future are incorrect. If people cannot predict their success, then it follows that others may not have been correct in predicting their failure. There is an additional sense of winning that comes from having been a longshot and coming in first.

Along these same lines of manipulative-like interventions for dealing with inmates displaying inadequacy is to request that they *pretend as if they were someone who can do the task*. Requesting someone to pretend gets rid of a lot of anxiety. Pretending is fun, not work. If we fail while pretending to be someone else, there is less damage to our self-esteem. It wasn't us who failed, but our interpretation of whomever failed.

A powerful statement that I have found useful directs the inmate with low self-esteem away from the inmate's ability and focuses on the inmate's desire. The statement intentionally is geared to hook the rebellious person's desire to rebel. Yet, if you look closely at the statement, a command has actually been issued. For example, in dealing with an inmate who has been lying about the work that has been done, the line could be used in this fashion, "I'm not convinced that you want to be honest about what you do," or "I'm not convinced that you want to do the work." When these statements are issued without a critical sound in our voice, they imply that the inmate needs to convince us. At the same time, there is a subtle command to be honest or to do the work.

In using statements like the above that seek to be directive or are manipulative, one must be cautious. When they are used to control someone for just our benefit, there is a heavy price, as any careful reading of the previous pages would detect. However, when we are skillful in helping the other person achieve his or her goals or raise that person's self-esteem, usually folks will go along with the ruse even though many can see through the maneuver. This type of less straightforward tactic does not take away the other person's ability, it simply returns power and ability that has been misplaced.

Being straightforward, honest, and open (unlike the above) is powerful when applied intentionally. Openly identifying with the inmate who is displaying inadequacy can be very effective. An incident that happened between a volunteer Bible study teacher and an inmate who lied constantly demonstrates this style of relating. The resident, whom I will call Sarah, lied about everything all the time. Her lies were the variety that are easily spotted and which are told to raise others' opinions. She lied about her age, her friends, her background whenever it was convenient or not. Out of my brilliance, I chastised her, sought to relate to her, forgave her, and simply confronted her whenever I detected a lie. The volunteer Bible study teacher was more effective. She pulled Sarah aside and said to her, "You know, Sarah, I, too, used to have a problem with lying, much like you do; and while I did, I felt terrible about myself and couldn't seem to stop." The volunteer went on to say how a friend had prayed with her about her lying and that she had been able to stop. She told about how she had gone around and straightened out the lies that she could remember having told. She then invited Sarah to pray with her like her friend had prayed with her. Sarah remained at KCIW for another four months and never again in my presence did she lie. Why was this prayer more powerful than any of the other prayers for Sarah to stop lying? I believe that one reason was that the Bible study teacher implied that she liked Sarah, and that if she was like Sarah, then Sarah could be like her. That isn't a lot different than what the Gospel says that Jesus did by simply living as all of us.

The above illustration demonstrates the use of the next option as well as identifying *telling stories about one's own failures*. Telling stories about your own failures communicates an important message which is, if I used to be like you, it follows that you can be like me now. This implies hope as well as concern, commitment, and interest, all of which are powerful and encourage hope.

Prescribing behavior or *requesting a behavior* are the same and are used to reduce anxiety. The principle of this technique is to prescribe the behavior that one is most likely to do and describe some reason for a person doing the task. For instance, in dealing with an inmate who frequently lies about not bothering to do work, we might request the behavior by saying, "Now if this task is too difficult for you, I want you to just sit down and not do it." By prescribing or requesting the customary behavior, we are inviting one's resistance to criticism to be operating for them rather than against them, because their desire to not admit that they can't do the work will prompt them to avoid their usual behavior. In the case above, the inmate would be likely to want to avoid having to face the fact that he is unable to do the job.

With people whom we know are overly sensitive to criticism and who have limited abilities, we can add a line to the directions which accepts our own responsibility such as, "If you get confused by my lack of clarity, please sit down and do nothing." By prescribing the behavior in this way, no matter what the inmate does, she or he is right.

Finally, religious folks have additional options. They can provide additional information to inmates operating from inadequacy about the guilt they have or their need to avoid criticism. The Gospel has positive ways of dealing with guilt or with our need to avoid criticism.

SUMMARY

How our attitude is important in determining the success with which we give back responsibility was one focus here. We also saw how our desire to return responsibility needs to be for the benefit of the other person and not a way to satisfy our own need. We discussed the different general "types" of inmates and the differences in returning responsibility to the different "types" of people.

We saw the value in asking questions and of saying the opposite of what everyone else has said. Finally, we discussed and explained the behavioral options from the behavioral option chart.

In the next section we will discuss the methods of taking care of ourselves in order that we might be able to continue applying the methods outlined above.

NOTES

[1] Irvin D. Yalom, *The Theory and Practice of Group Psychotherapy* (New York: Basic Books, Inc., 1980), p. 92.

[2] *The Interpreter's Dictionary of the Bible* s.v., "Folly."

[3] Ibid.

[4] Ibid.

[5] Weldon C. Fuller, "Life Scripts of Female Offenders at the Kentucky Correctional Institution for Women," dissertation, Louisville Presbyterian Theological Seminary, 1977, p. 50.

[6] Ibid., p. 51.

[7] Ibid., p. 51.

[8] *DSM III: Diagnostic and Statistical Manual of Mental Disorders*, 2nd edition (Washington, DC., 1981), pp. 317-318.

[9] Ibid., p. 317.

[10] Ibid., p. 318.

[11] Ibid., p. 318.

[12] Heinz L. Ansbacher and Rowena R. Ansbacher, *The Individual Psychology of Alfred Adler* (New York: Harper and Row Publishers, 1956), p. 423.

[13] Ben Bursten, M.D., *The Manipulator: A Psychoanalytic View* (New Haven and London: Yale University Press, 1973), p. 156.

[14] George F. Bennett, *When They Ask for Bread* (Atlanta: John Knox Press, 1978), p. 91.

[15] *The Bible*, Proverbs 29:9.

[16] Fredrick S. Perls, *Gestalt Therapy Verbatim* (New York: Bantam Books, Inc., 1974 [first printed by Real People Press in 1969], p. 47.

[17] Ibid., p. 38.

[18] *Webster's Dictionary*, s.v. "manipulate."

Chapter 5

TAKING CARE OF YOURSELF

THE PRINCIPLES of taking care of yourself have everything to do with your emotional well being. There are two phases to this process. The first has to do with ways we handle our feelings at the moment and in the immediate time after the conversation that left us with uncomfortable feelings. The second has to do with long-range methods of reducing stress while working in a correctional setting.

Our attitude is important in determining how successful we will be in taking care of ourselves. The more we see this as a part of our jobs, the more we can be intentional about doing it. What we tell ourselves in the privacy of our thoughts is important. If we use thoughts like, "I can't stand this anymore," "She makes me so angry," or "He drives me crazy," we are programming ourselves to feel like what we are telling ourselves. Furthermore, all of these types of statements imply that we are without the ability to change how we feel and that is simply a lie. We are more than emotional puppets dancing to the strings pulled around us. Often we choose statements like the above to show emphasis to others about our feelings. There is a cost. Over time our overemphasis programs our emotional response, and we begin acting as if our words are true. We then automatically get upset when we see the person that "makes me mad." I have wondered if that was what Jesus had in mind when he said in Matthew 5;37, "Let what you say be simply 'yes' or 'no'; anything more comes from evil."[1]

Using such phrases or thoughts to occupy our minds is a form of passivity, because it doesn't involve looking for a solution to the difficulty at hand. Replacing these negative thoughts with simple statements about what we are feeling at the time is one thing we can do. When angry, recognize and acknowledge that we are simply angry. However, there are many more options available to us, ones we have used and are currently using. Often we are not conscious of the many effective things that we do while protecting ourselves. Some of these options follow.

We can exaggerate the way that we feel inside of our own mind until we reach the ridiculous. At that point, it is much easier to stop the bad feelings because we can laugh at ourselves and the ridiculousness of the situation. There is nothing new about this approach. Ethnic groups have been using this maneuver to cope with discrimination and prejudice for centuries. Many Jewish comedians have capitalized on the ability to laugh their way to feeling good in spite of difficult circumstances. To use this variation of the ethnic coping skill, simply exaggerate any feeling or tendency to the extreme. In fact, use your imagination and enjoy your experience. Other variations include determining how many jokes you can make about the uncomfortable situation.

Use of our creativity is a key that involves changing something serious and painful into something playful and amusing, simply by what we tell ourselves about the experience or about how we treat it. There are other ways to use our mental time to be helpful. For instance, we can remember a time when we were effective. When we visualize as completely as possible or attempt to re-create the experience in our minds, we can often resurrect the feelings that accompanied the original scene. Take a minute and recall a favorite and memorable time. Start with whatever sensory mode that is easiest — that is, sight, smell, hearing, or touch. Most people can recall the tune of a favorite song and hear it whenever they want. Is the beach your favorite place? If so, can you see the waves coming in and hear the sounds of the ocean? If so, can you smell the sea? How do you feel when you give yourself that experience? If you feel the same after the exercise, as in the above, you probably didn't give yourself time to savor the exercise and the moment. In any event, you can recognize how this could be helpful—if you were an officer working in a cell block and unable to leave, although an inmate was being less than polite in her conversation to or about you.

Either of these approaches enables us to reduce our feelings of failure, hurt, etc., and provide an emotional distance from the uncomfortable feelings we were having. All of us do this sort of thing eventually; however, while mulling over what someone has said, we often have to work ourselves into putting the anger behind us, almost like Dorothy in the "Wizard of Oz." She could return to Kansas anytime she wanted, but simply didn't know that she could; therefore, she took the long road home. We can take a shortcut.

Another thing we can do is forgive the person who has said things that we allowed to hurt us. Jesus did a few things on the cross that could be helpful to us. He quoted scripture, prayed, and forgave the people who were crucifying him. Lots of people think that forgiveness is for the other person. I think that forgiveness benefits the person forgiving, although it may also benefit the other at some point. I believe that one reason that Jesus prayed for forgiveness of the people who were hurting him was for his benefit. While in excruciating pain, I believe Jesus was taking care of himself as he prayed for the forgiveness of those who were crucifying him. Prayer brings us in touch with resources that we possibly have not dreamed of. It enlists outside help and provides support, while usually bringing a different feeling and outlook. Forgiveness is one of the most powerful things we can do for ourselves.

Lots of people think that they cannot forgive another person, because they don't feel like forgiving that person. They regrettably believe that we must act on our feelings and that is not true. Our feelings tag along behind our thoughts and actions. If you insist on believing that you simply cannot forgive until you feel ready, then change, at least, your "cannot" to "will not," and take credit for your decision.

Making decisions is something we can do for ourselves in difficult times. We can, in fact, decide what we want to do next, to whom we want to tell our experience, and begin planning strategy for the next time. What this does is remove us from the immediacy of our feelings and allows us some emotional distance, as well as provide a means for problem solving.

Most of the above tactics are not really thought of as being assertive, and if we are using them to avoid becoming assertive, then we are kidding ourselves, unless we are willing to adopt a new stance. Most people instinctively know whether or not they have difficulty in being assertive. Many religious people believe that somehow being assertive is less than Christian. Their view of Christ is often a passive one, and in their attempt to follow Jesus, they also adopt a passive stance. Well, at least, they will defend their passivity with their image of Jesus.

A stance of passivity simply welcomes others to use us, walk over us, and manipulate us. Implied in the passive stance is our need to be liked. Passivity almost invites others to kick us and abuse us. The image I have of Jesus is a person incredibly assertive, not aggressive. Aggression seeks to take the rights of others. Assertion simply and firmly expects self rights. If you know that you need to become more assertive, there are lots of paperback books on the subject which deal effectively with encouraging assertive behavior.

Finally, during or immediately following an uncomfortable encounter, we can ask ourselves a powerful question. The question was given to me by one of my supervisors so that I could protect myself. The question is, "Do I really want to continue feeling _____ ?" The first time I heard this statement or used it, I thought how silly it was to think that a statement might help me change the way I felt. When I realized that I really did feel differently after asking myself the question several times, I became convinced of its power.

While getting angry and expressing our anger toward or to the person who has acted inappropriately may be an inviting gesture, it may also be a futile act that invites more misbehavior. Inmates acting out of a sense of revenge will likely be encouraged that they could make us angry, if they see our angry displays. It is true that folks who have been in abusive families may feel closer to us, if we show them our strong feelings of anger when they surface. However, inmates who are highly manipulative are likely to be encouraged to continue their manipulative behavior, if they see that they can get us upset.[2] It is also important that we drain our hostility with another professional rather than against the manipulative person.[3]

Long-range methods of taking care of ourselves involve dealing with the stress and maintaining supportive relationships with people who work in corrections and with those who do not. Essentially, this means keeping a healthy balance in our life by dealing with stress both physically and emotionally by our relationships.

One mistake which persons who work in corrections make is to believe that people unrelated to corrections cannot understand how they feel. All this belief does is to help alienate the officer who believes it. Of course, people who have been through similar situations can more quickly understand what we are talking about. Yet, to believe that people who haven't experienced a similar situation cannot empathize or understand is to say that we can't explain what we are feeling. However, to expect a spouse to be able to completely fill the desire we have to discuss our feelings or work with them is also self-defeating. Someone unrelated to the unique field of corrections is not likely to be able to give as reliable advice or insight into a particular problem as a person who works in corrections. That is true of many, if not most, professions today.

Stress and its effects on our health has become so widely discussed and reported that articles and seminars abound on ways of reducing stress effects. Four things which we can do for ourselves are: (1) recognize and admit that all people are afraid of something; (2) find our particular place in the system; (3) know our value in being the unique human being that we are; and (4) make time to do something just for ourselves.[4]

The methods and particular means of stress management are far too important to overlook, even though this document cannot cover the material. If you do not have an existing program of intentional behavior to reduce or cope with stress, now is the time to develop one.

Sometimes officers experiencing high levels of stress in corrections decide the only way to cope is to leave the job. An important finding by Carroll Brodsky in "Work Stress in Correctional Institutions," has a discouraging thought about the ability to reduce work stress simple by leaving corrections. Based on Brodsky's extensive study of correctional officers and stress on those who left, he says,

> Those who did leave their jobs, however, did not always achieve the cessation of the discomfort. Among the subjects in this study, symptoms diminished but did not always disappear, nor did the stress itself end when they left their jobs. The workers continued to be angry and depressed about their experiences.[5]

Irregardless of whether we stay or leave corrections as employment, finding long-range coping skills for stress management is important. I believe that any effective stress management system also involves our spiritual self. Long ago, God gave us one means of dealing with stress in the form of the Second Commandment, "Honor the sabbath day and keep it holy, as the Lord your God commanded you. . . ." (Deuteronomy 5:12).[6] Our private devotions, as well as our corporate ones, are important sources of replenishing our spiritual energy and physical energy as well.

While this book has stressed the importance of emotional safety by lowering stressful situations by coping skills, it doesn't address in depth the other areas of our vulnerability. We are also vulnerable physically, spiritually, socially, and professionally. These attacks can be more insidious and stem more from the environment of the prison setting. They don't come directly from particular inmates but from the overall atmosphere of incarcerated people.

Physically we are vulnerable in part because of relating with people who largely have substance abusing backgrounds. Studies have shown the direct correlation of the physical problems and diseases that attack persons who are in codependent relationships with alcoholics. These findings highlight the importance of self care. Being in daily contact with people who have abused substances takes a toll unless we practice self care. Part of that self care needs to be recognizing the characteristics of codependency. We need to be able to know when we are allowing in some subtle way our value or emotions to be determined by the inmates. Sometimes no matter what we do, it will seem like no inmate appreciates what we have done. Furthermore, they may blame us for all sorts of things happening that we have no control over. Having our emotional life in part determined by the institutional atmosphere may have a bearing on our health.

While I'm not aware of any study that has documented the above as being a direct cause that correctional officers have a shortened life expectancy, I believe that it is a real contributing factor. Just because we or someone in our family isn't chemically dependent doesn't insure us from the effects. Realizing and reminding ourselves of the bounds of our responsibility may have a very real health benefit.

Relating with inmates can take a toll spiritually as well as emotionally and physically. Spending one-third of our lives with inmates who have little regard for the law, rules, or for God can erode our values. We can become desensitized to offenses. As that happens it is easier for us to violate our own codes of conduct. Being constantly with people who do not share our spiritual values can lessen our commitment as well. Constantly hearing the excuses and rationalizations of immoral behavior can begin to erode on our values of lesser importance. The shift demands of corrections often makes regular attendance at a place of worship difficult at best. This, too, can erode our spiritual life drastically. We need to be fed spiritually.

Socially we can begin to feel like outcasts. When at parties, it is uncomfortable when people sometimes back up from us when we tell them what we do. Little things like prison jargon can begin to have an isolating effect when used in the larger society. If for no other reason, jargon isolates people into those who know and those who don't. It is easy to then generalize that people don't understand how corrections people feel. In addition, people not involved in corrections often have a very distorted view of what prison work is like. Sometimes those old movies that portray correctional employees as vicious, greedy, and immoral has had an effect. Social self care often means explaining what corrections is like today. It means being willing to let people know what we encounter and how professionally we handle ourselves.

Social self care also means monitoring how we might have changed from working in prison. I know that I am more skeptical or suspicious of others and situations than people not associated with inmates. I think self care sometimes means recognizing that where we work is going to have some subtle changes in the way we encounter people and to adjust for those changes.

We are professionally vulnerable. Not only are we accountable for our actions, but we can be set up. However, self care means maintaining our relationships with staff members. It is not enough to be doing our job. It is important to guard against what impressions we give other staff. Simple things like letting others know what we are doing and why, can be important in keeping open channels of communication between ourselves and other employees. Making sure that we have informed all the people who need to know some aspect of our work can lower the possibility of misunderstandings. For instance, if we have had a disagreement with another staff member and we are going to be talking with that employee's supervisor about an unrelated subject, our presence with the supervisor may be misunderstood. Covering ourselves is a means of self care. It lowers the possibility of inmates using the incident to place a wedge between other staff and us. Just finding out about some new required procedure from an inmate rather than staff is grating. I think corrections etiquette is informing others when our actions are likely to impact them.

SUMMARY

How our attitude is involved in taking care of ourselves was analyzed in this section. We also discussed common words and phrases that do not help us to take care of ourselves, as well as ones that do.

We say how powerful forgiveness can be in taking care of ourselves. We also covered such other short-range methods of care as deciding what we will do and who we will tell, being assertive, asking the question, "Do I really want to continue _____ ?" and handling our angry feelings.

In the long-range methods of taking care of ourselves, we say the importance of the following: keeping a healthy balance, our faith, and talking to others unrelated to corrections as well as people involved in corrections. We also discussed the importance of a strategy for dealing with long-term stress and our areas of vulnerability.

NOTES

[1] *The Bible*, Matthew 5:37.
[2] George F. Bennett, *When They Ask for Bread* (Atlanta: John Knox Press, 1978), p. 94.
[3] Ibid., p. 94.
[4] Ronald Black "Stress and the Correctional Officer," *Police Stress* (February, 1982), p. 15.
[5] Carroll M. Brodsky, "Work Stress in Correctional Institutions," *Journal of Prison and Jail Health*, Vol. 2, No. 2 (Fall/Winter, 1982), p. 79.
[6] *The Bible*, Deuteronomy 5:12.

Appendix 1

THEOLOGICAL FOUNDATION

MY THEOLOGY THAT the basis for this book is based upon the premise that God is One and by living as this we help ourselves. The more that we act and think with the belief that God is One, the less self-defeating problems we create or perpetuate. The idea that our fundamental problems come from our attempts to be or act more than a created being is not new and is held by some modern theologians as well.[1]

In a country that has "In God We Trust" on it's money, the above may sound elementary. Most Americans acknowledge verbally one god. However, often our actions do not indicate that we practice what we say we believe. In practice we often worship a multitude of gods.[2] We worship what others think about us, we worship the right image of ourselves, we worship favored emotion, in short we have a multitude of gods. I am thinking of worship as what we place our emphasis on or give high value to.

In whatever ways that we worship something other than God, we make ourselves vulnerable. Where we get our value and importance can also remove that importance. For instance, if our primary importance comes from our work then at retirement we no longer have much value. In whatever ways we worship certain responses from other people make us even more vulnerable. For instance, if you begin to sense that I have a large investment in not being seen as prejudiced, then you can easily maneuver me by my desire to not be seen as prejudiced.

Our beliefs affect the way that we experience and understand the attitudes that we employ toward situations and people. The attitudes are influenced by what we believe about the nature of sin, existence, evil, and God.[3] Thus the Ku Klux Klan understands differently the admonition of love one's neighbor than does the National Association for the Advancement of Colored People (NAACP), even though both groups might espouse and defend the same scripture to support their claim.[4] Even though we are not always aware of our divided allegiances, our gods are legion.

By placing our faith in truth, reality, our logic, or any other person, concept or group, we are worshiping someone or something other than God. We will worship someone or something whether we consciously decide to or not. Where we place ultimate value becomes the temple where we worship. It is impossible to not worship something. Whether we are atheist, agnostic, or Christian, we will have consciously or unconsciously chosen our ultimate value. The choice will be apparent in how we treat the world and in our decisions, and actions.

Our faith will also surface in where we experience fear. Any fear indicates what we value. As a consequence, what we really value can be different from what we say we value. The irony is that our fears drive us as much or more than our desires. The second irony is that what we fear often comes to us because that is where we have placed emphasis in our life.

It is the unspoken and unacknowledged fear that is the vulnerable part in us that invites bad feelings from others. For instance, if I fear being shunned by inmates then I am more vulnerable to issues of rejection by inmates. In all likelihood my fear will come true, because the fear will be sensed and utilized to manipulate me.

Our backgrounds and the environments have tremendous affect and effect on our lives. Yet, it is not our upbringing or environment that account for the consistent and continuing problems of people. It is our faulty belief system about our experiences that cause us difficulties.[5] How else can the phenomenon be described when two people suffer equally disastrous losses in their lives, while one becomes bitter and the other becomes even more secure and feels loved?

With all of this talk about fear, ultimate value can be also thought of as sin. If that line of reasoning is taken, then it could lead someone to believe that people with mental problems or just problems have brought those on themselves. Although this is partially true, it is good news. We cannot change the world, we can only change our responses to the world and the difficulties we face. This view can also be misinterpreted to be implying that someone who is sick mentally is a greater sinner than one who is not mentally handicapped. This is missing the point. The manner in which a person defends him/herself, or uses a particular manner of defense that results in neurosis, only allows us to recognize the manner in which that person more consistently sins in one particular fashion. That a person equally sinful does not have mental or emotional problems is only an indication that the person has more varied methods of protecting self from perceived threats. There is no basis for ascribing the level of sin to health or sickness. Most of us recognize that people are shaped by the sufferings they have gone through. We also recognize that it is the way that each person defines what they have experienced that shapes them as much as the actual experiences they have encountered.[6]

It is the manner in which we respond to the other person that indicates whether we are responding to the other person or a remembered or created entity or an it. That is if I relate to you in a manner that suggests that you have no right to choose or think certain thoughts then I have made you an it.[7] When I do that I have made myself a thing.[8] To the degree that I give freedom, I give myself freedom. Furthermore, the more willing I am for you to decide and think your own thoughts and respect those thoughts even though they are different from mine, then I can respect myself, and worship God more completely. In other words, if I need you to believe the way I do, then I am not worshiping God, and I am not respecting either of us.

Much of the material and all of the techniques listed in this book are designed to be inviting relationships that are mutually respecting. We get what we give. Granted, the techniques are canned in the sense that they are not spontaneous. However, in practicality we often need models to inspire our creativity. We also need patterns to structure our creativity in helpful ways.

Often we relate to people based upon our expectations of how they will relate to us from the ways they have related to us in the past.[9] No matter how accurate our expectations or predictions are, it is our unwillingness to recognize and allow for differences and changes that people undergo that helps fuel our making the other person into an it. In fact, it can be our expectations which lead to the predictions being accurate. Conversely, it can be that by responding differently ourselves that we invite the other person to begin to act differently toward us.

It is by relating in the present with authenticity that we can begin to reinterpret our past in different ways.[10] Thus it is through the reinterpretation of the past through events of our present action toward others that gives us the possibility of new options and freedom. It allows as well for an reinterpretation of the future through the present.[11] For instance, a woman who has been abused by males and who fears being abused may act with men in ways that invite bad feelings because of her fear. When she has the experience of relating to a male who is not abusive, she has increased her options. If all men are not abusive to her then it isn't her fault that she was abused. If on the other hand she doesn't encounter relationships with men that are not abusive, then she can never be as sure that it wasn't her fault.

Generally speaking we cannot often think ourselves into or out of problems, simply by thinking. In part, because a part of us always knows that we are the one talking to ourself. Yet new experiences can alter our perspectives where no amount of logic can.

For the manipulator, our relating with respect can have a moral influence. Because our authenticity can transcend their lived history and will become a part of their inner history.[12] Once I have had an experience of being accepted by you, I can never not have had that experience. It will become a part of my inner experience forever. It may also convict me of how I treat others. Your acceptance of me may subtly point out the difference between the way I want to be treated and the way I treat others.

Genuine repentance requires trust in a power greater than ourselves.[13] A power then can and will provide support. One ingredient in trust is acceptance. That is a feeling or sense that the other person values us and is not secretly demanding that we change in order to be accepted. This has been one of the principles stated in the book as well as the intention of the psychological messages that are produced by the interventions offered. For instance, humorous derailment may well cross a transaction to stop some unwanted and unhelpful attack or power struggle. Yet, one of the messages that can be recognized by this intervention is that the sender likes the second party enough to laugh with him/her. In a very real sense this is communicating acceptance.

All of the interventions are intended to be respectful or indicate value of both inmate and staff. Being respectful is the surest way of protecting self, because being disrespectful or making the other person into an it also violates ourselves and makes us more vulnerable to attack.

In summary, the First Commandment to have no other gods before us implies a direct bearing on the way we relate to each other, including the manipulators. Thus it means striving to relate to individuals rather than images or stereotypes that we create. By doing so we may not only experience an increased sense of self-esteem but also recognize God as being with us.

In practical terms this means we must hear both the verbal and unspoken messages and communicate on both levels as well. Yet our unspoken messages must in some way communicate self-respect and a willingness for the other person to be an individual. Furthermore, when we do this we are less likely to be relating to an image or demanding a specific type of response that limits the other's freedom, and ours as well. As a consequence, we, too, are freed from our images and are protected at least in part from the entangling web of the manipulator's self and other destructive behavior.

NOTES

[1] H. Richard Niebuhr, *The Responsible Self* (New York: Harper and Row Publishers, 1963), p. 132.
[2] H. Richard Niebuhr, *Radical Monotheism and Western Culture* (New York: Harper and Row Publishers, 1940 and 1960), p. 24.
[3] Niebuhr, *Responsible Self*, p. 124.
[4] Niebuhr, *Radical Monotheism*, p. 34.
[5] Niebuhr, *Responsible Self*, p. 59.
[6] Ibid., p. 59.
[7] Martin Buber, *I and Thou* (Edinburg: T&T Clark, 1937, 1952), p. 4.
[8] Ibid., p. 4.
[9] Niebuhr, *Responsible Self*, p. 101.
[10] H. Richard Niebuhr, *The Meaning of Revelation* (New York: Macmillan Publishers, 1941 and 1960), p. 5.
[11] Niebuhr, *Responsible Self*, p. 104.
[12] Niebuhr, *Meaning of Revelation*, p. 62.
[13] Craig Dykstra, *Vision and Character: A Christian Educator's Alternative to Kohlberg* (New York: Paulist Press, 1981), p. 92.